ANGELINA AT THE SERRANO

Andrea Lambert

ISBN: 978-81-19654-37-6

First Edition: 2024
Rs. 200/-

Cyberwit.net
HIG 45 Kaushambi Kunj, Kalindipuram
Allahabad - 211011 (U.P.) India
http://www.cyberwit.net
Tel: +(91) 9415091004
E-mail: info@cyberwit.net

Printed at Repro India Limited.

Chapter 1 — LEAVING SAN FRANCISCO

I was so tired of working so hard. Constantly being tired and hungry.

I got off the N-Judah train. Stopped in a cafe. Considered moving home to my parents house in San Diego. Their five-bedroom, three-bathroom suburban house seemed like a sanctuary. It was so cold in San Francisco.

I might be done. Trying to make it on my own. If this was what it took. It seemed kinder this way. Harm reduction. Why not move home? Clean up? Go to graduate school? Get one of those MFA's Dave talked about. Work on those novel manuscripts I'd discarded.

Limone moved out. I got lonely. Went to Reno for Christmas. Spent the return trip thinking about how nice it was to eat enough. I wasn't willing to steal, even when I was starving. I was slowly starving, as the temp jobs dried up.

I felt less and less welcome in my usual nightlife haunts.

While I was out of town for Christmas, Dave kicked Angelina out. She moved in with Billy.

My father picked me up at 7 am on a Sunday.

The first thing I said was, "Can we get something to eat?" My bank account was overdrawn. Both of my credit cards maxed out. I spent all of my money on drugs. On people who weren't my friends anymore. I was humiliated. I was 29.

I stepped into the red minivan. A failure. Watched my whole world disappear in the rear view mirror. I knew I had to leave San Francisco. It was just time to go. Everyone knew I had herpes. There was no one left to sleep with. I had no more money. I couldn't work any more. I was sick. Physically. Mentally.

I didn't tell my parents that I was a drug addict.

I only said, "I lost my job." That was true. I lost two full time jobs. Couldn't get enough temp work.

San Francisco was too expensive. I couldn't support myself there anymore. Warhookers went belly up a month before I left. I didn't tell the few people I met in San Diego that I was running away from being a drug addict.

I kept my addictions a secret. I kept so many other secrets. For so many years.

This writing is fiction. It is not secret. All of this is imaginary. It exists on the page. In a world. A word. You enter, as you turn the page.

Valley of the Dolls before bed at my parents house. Woke up with one arm twisted behind my neck and the other groping madly at the air in my childhood waterbed. Transferred the SOMA magazine subscription to my parents house. Savored each chic glossy page. Of a world I didn't live in anymore.

I came to San Francisco after shedding my youth in Portland. I became a temp, another type of secretary. I wore suits. Traipsed around the Financial District in heels.

Dionne Warwick sang on the *Valley of the Dolls* soundtrack, "Got to get up. Got to get out. Time to find life on my own. Got to get up. Got to get on. Got to get off of this ride. Got to get got to find. Need to get hold of my pride."

I was alone for most of the next year. 2005 was a sad year. I was alone in my parent's house with them oblivious to the withdrawals that consumed me. The daily vomiting that I tried to drown with even more of their wine.

Sitting on the balcony of their suburban home. Painting my toenails teal blue. Staring blankly at the phone that never rang. Reading all of the Harry Potter books. Lingering in Barnes and Noble with my mother.

My father put me to work night and day in his office. I cooked the entire South Beach Diet cookbook for my parents. Worked in my father's law office as a file clerk. Was essentially an indentured servant for a year.

I was thankful my parents took me in. They saved me. I had nowhere to go.

Summer 2005, I began to work for my father. He was a lawyer. His office was a cramped, 100 degree basement bedroom in my parent's house. Fifties thermodynamics textbooks and TORT restrictions lined the walls. Four stacks of Acco-bound pleadings. Inscrutable documents.

I climbed the stepladder in a halter top. My parent's house didn't have air conditioning. They bought it in the 1970's. Before global warming.

My father said, "The breeze comes in from the ocean." We weren't far from the beach. La Jolla. It's elegant coastline was next door. On the other side of the 5 and 52 freeways.

I wrote practice GRE essays about driving along the La Jolla coastline. Carried thick legal documents. The owners manuals to every electronic device my father ever owned. Up five feet. Down five feet.

I am five four. Even in heels. Professional accoutrements such as heels were chucked working for Dad. I couldn't see above the forth file drawer. There were six. More files in the back bedroom. Files in the garage.

For some people, filing is a myth. For others a necessity. For my father, filing was a passion. I became sucked into this passion. I had no car. Couldn't get an outside-the-house job, at first. I was afraid to call my old temp agency.

I sweated through my blouse. Hole punched until my vision swam. Everything had to be Acco-ed. That is to say, bound at the top with a two-prong metal thing. The files had to be pinched open. At exactly the one-inch mark. No more. No less. I made about five hundred files this way.

The Acco's created the problem.

My father leaned over from his swivel chair on a cracked plastic mat. His great weight wheezed in a pair of khaki shorts.

"You've got these all wrong," he said. "The holes are supposed to go a half-inch to the right. You need to do these all again."

Many of these legal motions went to Exhibit Z.

My father told me the plan, "Go through with the scotch tape. With every sheet lay a strip of tape along the top. Punch the holes again. The file folder too. File them on the third top file drawer to the left."

I couldn't do this anymore.

To raise cash to move out, I took a temp job.

Pathways Personnel again. They placed me at a nonprofit. International relief work. I tried so hard get hired. They kept me on as a temp for nine months. This way they didn't have to give me health insurance. I was easier to fire.

I saw *Rent* with my mother in San Diego. Cried from the beginning credits.

Brady told me before he died, that he thought *Rent* romanticized the virus. His wasted limbs piercing through tight trousers. A tin of government peanut butter from the food bank in his hands. He was HIV+. I was afraid I was also.

Rent portrays a group of edgy musicians, strippers, and filmmakers. In 1980s New York. Before the more effective antiretrovirals. Death was assured and harsh. *Rent* wrenched the fragile joy of short lives lived fully. Emotive. Tender. Gorgeously performative. Possibly manipulatively tear-jerking. The cruelty of the virus.

In San Diego I was far away from San Francisco. Anyone who used to be a friend, Brady was dead. Lucas was homeless. No one called me anymore. Party people had bigger problems. Or they didn't have enough cell phone minutes. To listen to me.

AIDS brackets my life. Haunted me. I cried in my parent's guest bedroom. AIDS fear pursues me. A ghost. A lingering presence.

My mother. Next to me in the movie theatre. Teared up a bit. We left the bathrooms. She asked me why I cried so much. I couldn't tell her. I didn't want to tell her. I told her imperfectly what I could.

"*Rent* reminded me of San Francisco." I said. "The friends I left behind,"

I got the idea to go to go to Cafe Bassam downtown. To work on *Jet Set Desolate.* Attempt to be approachable through careful wielding of mid-drift and manuscript. It was a long drive from University City. To downtown San Diego. To dubious, caffeinated results.

What did I expect? To meet someone I could date? Who would be willing to date someone who lived with their parents? Unlikely. I lost my nerve. Stayed home with a bottle of Vanilla Smirnoff. I didn't know who I was anymore. Now that I wasn't the party slut. Who always had coke. A skeleton key.

I steeped in isolation. 2005. More and more difficult to go out. Easier to stay home. Where I was comfortable. Safe. I could listen to my old San Francisco music. Remember. Write. My sole passion these days.

I curled up in the pedicure chair. I bought it with Jesse. In the Tenderloin. In*Jet Set Desolate.* I carted it back to San Diego in Dad's minivan. The one piece of furniture I'd been able to take with me. That chair was all I had left. I'll never throw that vinyl chair away. The cats clawed it near to bits. Every partner I've had since wanted me to get rid of it. I never will. I love its mid-century modern lines.

I woke up at 7:30 am. Worked all day. Went to a non-profit where they paid me eleven dollars an hour. I researched customs regulations on the Internet. Why someone lost a package of "The L Word." DVDs they were trying to ship to our field office in Honduras.

WTF? You can't track the USPS! I don't know what happened to your goddam DVDs! I mean, if I'd had the presence of mind to FedEx them this wouldn't have happened, but I'm told to cut corners and be cheap so we can feed more babies in Ethiopia, so I sent it priority mail and they completely vanished off the face of this earth. I'm sorry. Stop calling me about it, I need to get my eyebrows done. And, no, I don't know if the hotel in Malawi has a view.

Things I wanted to say to my co-workers that I stuffed.

I was under a lot of stress. Felt trapped. I needed to get out of my parents house. I applied to a seven grad schools that winter. Hoped one of them would rescue me. Take me off to a place where I just had to produce vivacious text. About my sordid life. Live in a garret. With a bed. Somewhere.

The water mixes with coconut oil. Becomes a fire. I am burning even now. I am a phoenix. Burning in light and darkness. In the glory of my exploitation. I am on fire.

Chapter 2 — GOLDEN HILL

I was ready to live on my own. Ten graduate school applications sent out. Ten schools. One of whom I hoped to attend. For an MFA program. Ten hopes. I would take any of them. One final option still fluttering out of reach. I wanted that MFA.

I moved into a shared apartment in Golden Hill. My mother took a photograph that day. I stood against the wall. My face tilted sideways. One arm behind my back. The other free at my side. The *Valley of the Dolls* record cover visible behind me. The cellophane sleeve caught the light. Sent tendrils of iridescence across the pink boudoir on the sleeve.

Behind me was a painting. A women in a slip. Sunglasses. A martini glass in sharp relief. A queen of spades. A shot of a downtown Portland stairwell. Layer upon layer of typewritten text against the body. The curtain. The shadows of her clavicles. A canvas. I hauled it from Portland. To San Francisco. Now to the Golden Hill neighborhood of San Diego.

The walls of my new apartment was white and clean. The red silkscreen on my shirt was stretched and worn. My eyes were clear. By now my arms were clean of yellow-purple tracks. My nose hairs were growing back. I felt that I might be able to refuse the offer of a line. Perhaps. Probably. If offered by a future dorm-mate.

Alone that night. Bits and drifts of the past. I held my feet together. Pushed back the top of the sheet. Ants. Spiders. My air mattress was shoved on a corner. Spider webbing below and above.

If not now, when? When would life begin again? I got out of bed. Pulled upright through the humid air. Global warming. The ceiling fan whirred impotently. Shoved the hot air around in little circles. Bars on the high windows showed bougainvillea and ferns.

All I could do was write *Jet Set Desolate*, now. All I could do was sit in front of the old Dell desktop that I'd dragged back from San Francisco. Pour out all of the memories. Blood beads around needles. Lines of speed done off of Beat Happening CDs.

Nothing was happening here except me. Waiting. In this little apartment I shared with an uncommunicative guy. Waiting for my life to start. Walking past the neighbor's houses.

I drove to work in a 1979 Oldsmobile. My grandmother left it to me. Sat in the hot velour back seat on my lunch break. Scribbling out how my life had been once. How I'd grabbed risk. Desire. Pain. Been poisoned right out of town.

Walking down the alley behind the apartment complex, the smells hit me first. The smell of red meat. The luxuriant steak smell from the Turf Club. Blanketing the intersection in blood. Then the heat and flowers woven together. Interlocking.

The heat bled into flowers as I traipsed down the sidewalk. Vodka under my arm. A greasy bag of tamales in my hand. From Ernesto. At the corner stand. On 25th and C. Big coolers with steaming pork, green chili and pineapple. Hot pineapple tamales were the "it" snack that summer.

I thought about tamales. Turnedthe corner into Jarocco's Market. From the corner of my eye I caught a stubby homeless guy gesticulating. Demanding rum. Demon rum.

I am alone.

I went back to my new apartment in Golden Hill. Crazberry Boru vodka. $9.99 on sale. Put it in a tall blue glass with lemonade.

The screen door shoved open, slightly. Someone tapped.

I heard, "Lena!" My neighbor friend Micah tiptoed in the door. He dropped in after work. I had alcohol.

Micah slid off his sunglasses. Slumped onto the blue canvas couch. His seersucker pants were bleached out fresh. He pulled off his straw hat. Set it on the battered desk with the record player and the Manchester chimes. A purple-bobbed mannequin head watched us from the corner vantage point. Three malnourished fish twined from the tank.

I asked, "How's things."

"Dreadful. It's so tragic. My therapist won't push through my disability. I don't know if I'm going to make rent."

"Cocktail?" The blare of the ferns outside iced with sun.

"Oh! Darling!"

I padded. Barefoot. Nails cracked and infected to the narrow kitchen. Warped cabinets filled with empty Trader Joe's bags warred with flies. In the cabinets cut blue glassware from the Tenderloin Goodwill. I selected two champagne flutes. Pulled the cranberry vodka from the freezer. Tossed it with lemonade. Topped each with a strawberry. I ambled around the corner to where Micah sat with his arms upwards.

We felt fabulous, Micah and I. Fabulous in our poverty. In our beauty and disease.

"The Evita?"

"Oh, Doll. Thank you. I needed a little drinksie."

"Oh, me too. It's been one of those slow days of hell. The little death. The heat."

"110 in New York. Don't get me started."

"Grandma won't leave her house. Reno's at 102 degrees. She has A/C. She figures that's all she needs. She won't go grocery shopping.

She's run out of Aleve. I want to send her a care package with some popsicles and Codeine."

"Bad back?"

"Bad hips." At this, I got up. Flicked on the ceiling fan. It spanned the living room with a wash of cool air. We sat on the blue IKEA couch with the slip-covers half-off. The pillows scattered.

Paintings from the former tenants on the walls. My *Valley of the Dolls* record cover. A black lace fan I picked up in Chinatown. My roommate's broken end table covered with skate stickers hunkered to the left.

I slumped down on the couch next to him. Set my vodka on the table. Micah leaned back.

"Ah, that is so much better." He ran a hand through his salt-dashed hair. "Do you think I should cut it? I mean, do you really think so? I just don't know. It's just not Versace enough."

"Versace what?"

"Oh, I didn't tell you. Yeah, I used to be a Versace model in Miami. Back in the eighties. Print. Not runway. I was too short."

"Oh, how fabulous for you," The bars on the windows rattled as a police car squealed by. I watched the red stripes as they sliced his face to disco ribbons. "How was Versace?"

"Oh, I suppose. It was all you would imagine, but then the bubble got old. It's like you have your bubble."

"This is my bubble. I have my apartment. It's my bubble. I leave for wine, toilet paper and tamales. That's it."

"That's it?"

"Oh, yeah, to go to work."

"Pesky, that."

He drew his hands around his body like a dewdrop.

"In the bubble."

"Yes, I'm in the bubble."

"Could you, dear," he gestured with the glass.

"Yes, dear. It's all in the bubble."

"Now, outside of the bubble? Do you? Would you? Could you? Know where to get some… Dare I ask…?"

"You mean...?"

"Coca?"

"Micah! You know I don't. I… I wish I did. The only dealer's numbers I have are in San Francisco. We're in San Diego. Its a teensy bit too far to go."

"Of course not. Oh! We couldn't, no. Ah well."

Shambling. Drunk. I fell into the hibiscus bush. Outside my lime green building. Buildings lined A Street. Until the City College marked the beginning of downtown. Until the I - 5 marked the last exits to the Mexican border. I lifted myself slowly, as Micah lifted my other arm.

Alcohol ruined my life for 20 years. But oh, for that glorious summer of 2005 drinking was wonderful. Micah and I would escape into a dream world. Where we painted beauty down for filth. At the wrought iron table on my lanai. Under the jasmine. A bottle a day we shared. Sometimes two. Drinking glorious white wine in the late afternoon. Fading warmth as we talked. Remade the world with us as kings and queens.

"I, I would be king, and you, you would be queen," David Bowie sings in *Heroes*

"Whoa, Nellie," Micah said. He righted me.

I picked a red hibiscus. Placed it resolutely behind one ear.

A video artist named Mike Kelley said, "I make art to give other people my problems."

The books I write are my way of giving my problems away to the world. Page after page.

Hot days on the lanai. Late nights in the stifling bedroom.

A door opened inside my mind. Late at night. As I slept. I passed through and up and out past the miasma of my dream. Into the cold shock of my sheets. The white linen stained. Rumpled over my naked shoulders. One arm out. One arm in. Both eyes open. Staring. Straight upwards.

I heard a man clearing his throat. A mucosal gag by the kitchen. In the bathroom. I heard a man's voice. Doors opening and closing as if my medicine cabinet was being ransacked. Forgotten beauty creams, Advil and razors were all that were in there. I stared straight ahead into the plaster spanning my ceiling. The dark hollows of my bookshelf. The living specter of my computer that I prayed would not arch to some electromagnetic fruition and come to life.

I was alone in my Golden Hill apartment. With the puppet from Bali Brady gave me hanging on the wall. Huddled silent in bed. My eyes moved frantically back and forth. The terror ricocheted.

I heard a door in my apartment open. It closed. Thumping. Shuddering. An echo. A bang that seemed to go on into another bang and another. Another door closed, loudly. I realized it was the front door. The intruder left.

An hour passed. Two hours. Three hours. My pinwheel pinhole eyes nailed to the ceiling slats. I froze in terror or half-sleep. The shade of dawn outside. It got brighter. Morning came.

The sweat and terror came back. I knew I had to run. I rose in the dark. Fumbled for the pants and blouse I laid out for work. I pulled them on. Pelted out the door.

I glanced around the dark patio. Dew glistened in cobwebby ferns. The sallow promise of begonias. The gargoyles of the hibachi. I turned. Set one foot ahead of another through the garden gate. Underneath the ivy arch. Down the cobble-stoned path marked by puddles. Along the sidewalk where ants and hibiscus thrust sharp stalks and rot.

The pit bull in the corner house threw itself bodily against the chain link fence for all that it was reinforced with scrap lumber. The neighbors kept a kiddy-pool for the cur to bathe.

I jetted off the curb. Across the street to Micah's gate. His apartment complex was gated like I wished ours was. Micah and his boyfriend Timothy lived in the center tower. The Evita apartment as he called it. Two Spanish-style buildings full of teenage Sea World acrobats flanked them.

It was a peach of a courtyard with their central tower. French doors opening onto a balcony. I rang the doorbell. Yelled Micah's name. My voice was loud in the courtyard. On the grass. The stucco and brick. Echoing damp to the moon.

Chapter 3 — POLICE

Morning. On his boyfriend's orders, Micah and I shuffled down the street. Into a Starbucks. The dawn light was gray as a mug shot. Brown panel hotel art. Canned jazz framed the corner storefront. Micah turned to me, "Lena, you know I don't have - "

Micah never had any money. He was on disability. I had an entry-level office job.

"It's okay, it's on Project Concern. They gave me a $20 Starbucks card for Secretary – pardon me – Administrative Professionals Day. I can only drink so much coffee. I need to talk to you. I'm so fucking scared. My god! They… They...."

He put a hand on my arm. "It's okay, Lena. For me a chai latte. Decaf. Okay? On you?"

"Okay. Okay."

He ordered for us. I paid. Before our drinks arrived, he led me to an overstuffed chair in burgundy velvet. I sat. He sat across from me.

"You have to file a police report. You know that, right?"

"The police? My God, no!"

"Lena. Lena. Get a hold of yourself. They are not going to hurt you. This time you have not committed any crimes. They don't know about any of that old stuff. To them you are Lena Cosentino. Nonprofit secretary. Author. Upright member of society."

"But I – " I knew there were old grains of cocaine in disco purses tucked away. Tucked in drawers for the party that might never come again. I would sit and dig with my finger to lick the dust. Get ever so slightly high again. I stored so many reckless tiny bags in that red croc skin clutch that the fabric was saturated.

If the police entered my bedroom? If they brought dogs? How could the police not know I used to be a drug addict? This would be the end.

"I can't."

"You have to file a police report," Micah said. "There might still be people inside your apartment right now, waiting for you to come back. They might kidnap you or worse. Lena. I worry for your safety. Please, call your parents tonight. Tell them about this. But first, before you go back into your house, you must send the police in there to make sure its safe."

"That means I would have to call them right now. I have to go to work today. I mean, I think I'm going to call in sick today and go see my psychiatrist. I need something much stronger for this anxiety."

"Does your work know you're…?"

"Bipolar? Ha! No, they don't even know I have tattoos. Mental illness is like instant firing. Sure, there's the Americans with Disabilities Act, but no one enforces it. No one believes me. I've lost so many jobs. After being institutionalized. Or admitting that I had to take a sick day to see my psychiatrist. There's no winning, either way, I just have to lie and lie. Hope I can keep this job, until I go away to school. Where I can at least be more honest about my condition. They can't throw you out of grad school for being crazy if you're medicated and manageable. I don't think."

"Lena, Micah?" The girl at the counter said, pushing across two steaming cups with green straws.

"Oh Hallelujah." Micah picked them both up. Brought me my drink. He sipped his daintily. "So, listen. Call them from here. We can start walking back. I'll stay with you."

At the corner of 24th and B Street, I watched the police car slow to a stop. Four officers got out. Four. No dogs. I clenched Micah's hand. He squeezed it. Let it go. The palm trees and hibiscus hedges were gray-green. The overcast sun drifted towards eight am.

I put one foot forwards then back.

One of the officers checked his notebook and advanced towards me,

"Are you Lena Cosentino?" He barked.

"Um... Yes?"

"Well, are you?"

"Yes. Yes I am."

"Is this your boyfriend?"

"Oh, no. He, ah, he has a boyfriend. I mean no."

The man peered at me under his black cap. "Okay..."

"Do you live here at 2457 B Street, apartment 3?

"Yes. Yes I do."

"Now, can you tell us what happened last night?"

I launched into a retelling of the previous nights events. Saw the cop's eyes narrowing under the black brim of his cap. I whined, babbling faster. Shrill. Female.

Finally he said, "Alright, that's about as much as we need to hear. Listen, we're going to go in there. Check it out. See if there's anyone in there. See what's missing. Make sure it's safe for you, alright?"

"Thank you, officer."

He half-smiled for a moment. I stared bleakly at the leering, open gate to the lanai. There were thick, dark footprints in the mud. Bigger prints than my feet or Micah's. I began to shake.

I didn't stopped shaking until the first policeman had entered that half-open porch gate. The racing thoughts only accelerated when they came out. Guns at the ready. Reported that my TV, iPod, blender and speakers were missing. There was also the matter of the flour and sugar strewn all over the carpet.

Later that day, the security guard at the Douglas Young Community Mental Health Clinic ran his metal detector up and down my body.

"Now open your bag, doll," he said. They always searched my bag before I went into the clinic.

I looked up at the Narcotics Anonymous flyers. Men's drum circle. Bi-polar Anorexics Anonymous. All the flyers yellow with rainbow-arced writing from the print shop Tahoma 48 point.

I opened my bag. Pulled out notebooks. That Franklin-Covey planner. Stuffed some queer bondage porn back into the ripped lining of my tote bag.

My psychiatrist worked at a public, low-income city clinic. In Mira Mesa. A beauty school across the courtyard. Only pigeons.

I was here at the county clinic. This time, to ask for a sedative. A Mother's Little Helper. In addition to my usual pharmaceutical cocktail. The break-in really stepped up my anxiety.

A couple sat across from me in the waiting room. Reading Esquire and Jane. The walls were irregularly hung with flyers for group homes. A bio-social support group for Schizophrenics that was cancelled until further notice. Flyers for warm lines. Multi-lingual crisis lines and more. A man with a shaved head and broad shoulders wedged into a flight jacket argued with Dr. Montoya as to whether or not he had to see her.

"It's all a mistake," the man said. He pawed through the pile of magazines. "All this shit I don't need," he said.

The woman in the chair shied away. Exhaled.

A pair of gothic teenagers bled one ring tone into another. The boy in a Joy Division shirt. The girl in purple plaid pants. I smirked into my Esquire. A bedazzled flip-flop swatted at me. I cringed. Word Finders and Sudoku on the floor.

The blithe woman in reception looked up from her day planner. She pulled back the sliding Plexiglass window. Separating her from the insane. Bulletproof. With a timid hand, she leaned out.

"Are we happy, people?" said the receptionist. "Is everybody happy?"

I put down the article on would you sell your wallet, your puppy, or your wedding ring for $1,000. I would but I only had one out of three. I followed Dr. Montoya down the hall. Sedatives. Bingo.

I felt the warm click of the needle fall to the record before I heard the whoosh of sound. The rising dulcet tones of the *Valley of the Dolls* soundtrack. Patty Duke as Neely O'Hara came on.

She sang, "Try my friend, to face yourself, with all you have in store."

I turned to Micah on the couch. He sipped the Two-Buck-Chuck that I had bought.

"Brace yourself… and give a little more..."

Micah looked up at me through thick eyebrows threaded with white.

"How was your shrink?" Micah said.

"Don't remind me. I did get the pills, though."

"Are they any good?"

Neely O'Hara sang, "And strike a brand new pose,"

"I haven't tried. Do you want one?"

"Sure, darling." He smiled.

From Neely, "With blues, you can't ignore..."

I hopped gleefully into my room. Got the pill bottle from my bedside table. Pressed the white plastic lid. I twisted it. Passed Micah an Ativan.

"They're prescription. Supposed to be a nice heavy sedative. Controlled substance, they said."

"Oh really? Fantastic."

"Oh yes." He took his. Leaned back along the sofa. Watched the fish twine and loop their way among the plastic seaweed. "So did that dastardly robber take anything?"

"Yeah. A bunch of my stuff is missing, I'm really pissed. He took my iPod. That little TV I had. The coin jar on the mantle with all my laundry quarters and – get this – my blender!"

"How odd."

"Yeah! He trashed the place too, as if that wasn't enough. He emptied the sugar and flour canisters into that shitty living room carpet. I mean, as you can see, I tried to vacuum. There's a deposit I may never see again. My roommate was pissed when he got back. Then he said he wasn't even sure I hadn't imagined the whole thing."

"Sure, that old inspired heart ain't all it was before," Neely sang, "But my friend, that tired heart, must try it's best to soar."

I looked down at my hands. Sat down next to him. Slipped the pill into my mouth. Swallowed brusquely, waterless. I hoped this would give me the calmness that I desperately wanted. My unquiet heart.

The trauma stacked like tinder. A fire started. I would burn possibly to ashes, to ruin.

Our heads reflected in the dark windows. Light. Shadow. The pearl dome of the clock's glass globe. Against the dark palms outside.

Hours later, we navigated the alley to 25th Street and Jarocco's Discount Market. A long silver twine of water. Ran down the central ditch. Marked with leaves and silt. Reflecting red from the stoplights. Punctuated with broken glass. We padded on either side. Bleary. Micah needed a cigarette. We heard bits of Mexican radio. A maternal voice rising with a child's cries. Pink stucco walls and window-bars on either side. A vine with red trumpet-flowers twined along a chain link fence. Blue plastic recycling bins on both sides. A profusion of flies. The air was thick and warm. The humidity wrapped us. In a bubble of Ativan gold.

At the brick house in the corner we turned right. With a quick glance over to Micah's shuttered place we aimed towards the bright door of the market. A hand-lettered sign claimed, "Wine Special: CK Mondavi - $3.99. Merlot-Cab-Chardonnay-Zinfandel." Another: "All milk: $1.25."

The pink neon horseshoe of the Turf Club radiated two doors down. The blood heat of the steaks palpable. An indistinct crowd circulated in front. But not for us. We didn't have the money for steak. It just wasn't on the menu. I had money for wine and wine only. Priorities.

Micah and I stopped short. Went into Jarocco's. A wall of liquor warred with smoked almonds. Red guppies in urine sample cups. The fluorescent lighting washed us out to wraiths. We dredged through the aisles. In search of a Riesling and some Camel Lights.

Micah opened the cooler door. Pulled out a blue bottle.

"Does this one look okay?" he said.

"How much is it?"

"It's okay. I'll get it. My disability went through."

"You're a doll. I don't get paid till next week. What's your disability for, anyway? If you don't mind me asking?"

"Depression. I'm HIV+. Plus, I'm blind in one eye."

"What? Micah! I'm... I'm so sorry."

"Don't be ridiculous." He looked away, than looked back at me. His mouth softened.

"Here," he opened his arms. I fell into them. Held him. As if he might break.

The fluorescence caught us in a silver glare. Struck off the cooler handles. Over the Canada Dry. Along the one shot bottles of SKYY vodka. Through the grating. Along the window. A police car siren came squealing past us with a red flare.

We sat on the patio on chairs. Mingling with ferns and spider webs. The heady bloom of the bougainvillea loomed behind the birdbath. I poured us each a glass of wine. Lit the candles. I felt warm and loopy. The Ativan took effect. Three glasses in. I began to veer and fumble. My words traced circles around Micah's fey exclamations. My eyelids drooped.

"Honey," he said. "You need to go to bed. Call me tomorrow, okay?"

I started. "But come on, not yet. Not now. Have another. We were only just starting to talk.

"Oh... Well, okay."

I poured. A car sped through the lonely street. It's red tail-lights reflected on the courtyard walls. Rev of the motor. The flutter of the candle's shadows against the stucco walls. They were cast in outline. Traced with ivy. Bound with the shuddering drone of an airplane above.

"No, really," Micah said. "I've got to go. Timothy will be worried. I wouldn't want to worry his pretty little head about anything. You'll be fine tomorrow. Get some rest." He picked up his sunglasses from where they were folded on the table. His thick fingers firm.

"No. Stay!"

"You're acting like an infant. Just put your little head on the pillow and rest. I mean it, darling." He narrowed his eyes at me.

"Fuck you, Micah."

"Go to bed." He turned. Walked towards the gate. "I'll call you tomorrow."

I picked up the blue flutes. Strode back into the kitchen. The empty weight of my apartment hung around me in humid waves. I was alone here in San Diego. Unlike busy San Francisco. Apart from the dubious consolation of my office job, my neighbor Micah was my only friend. Now, I knew he was dying.

I poured Micah glass after glass of wine. Hope he would talk to me in my isolation. I didn't even think that I was taking him away from his boyfriend. Who he lived with. Who supported him. I thought only of myself.

All could do was wait. I knew how to wait. I spent all my time waiting. Waiting for the grad school letters. Seven of them rejections so far. Writing into the void of my hard drive. Hoped that someday I would finish the endless book. I had three hundred pages of worn out disco trash. Some of it became *Jet Set Desolate.* Parts of it became *Neon Hysteric.*

I worried that this was all there would be. I could spend some interminable amount of my future. Stuck in San Diego. Spinning my wheels. Drinking vodka on the porch. Rotting into amnesiac silence.

I wiped a hand down the side of my face. Looked at the colander handing over the sink. The murky bruise-blotches on the basin. The moldy aquamarine tile. My single plate in the dollar-store dish rack. I sighed. Walked towards the cracked wood paneling of the hall.

Chapter 4 – BROKEN GLASS

Spider webs above and below. Cracks spread through my tiny apartment. Under my blow-up mattress. Like a rock never to be lifted. I sprawled on the bed. Legs thrown across the white sheets. I closed my eyes. Breathed in the quiet of the night.

I opened my eyes. Stared at the low red light on the white suitcase by my side. A sewing machine suitcase from Grandma Virginia. I kept my CDs in the suitcase. What few I hadn't sold for drug money. I set on the suitcase a succession of alarm clocks. Books. Water glasses. In my previous life, condoms.

I called Marith. A friend from Portland. Snap of the static come to life.

"Hey, just like you to call at midnight." She laughed. Still in Portland. Where I used to live. In Portland, with my heart. Friends. Soul. Volition. I longed for those halcyon, golden days. Beer on the porch. Summer sun.

"Is there something wrong with that? I'm sorry. You're probably sleeping."

"No, no. Getting ready to go out, actually."

"I'm getting ready to go to sleep, but I'm not sure if I can."

"You?"

"No, I'm just anxious. I'm afraid someone is going to break in again."

"That's legit. Just remember to breathe."

"Right. My shrink told me I should do breathing exercises and cut down on the coffee, but I don't know. They gave me these pills. They're sort of helping."

"Micah didn't stay over? He should stay with you. Or invite you over. Or something?"

I sighed. "No, he has Tim. His boyfriend. Who he lives with. He's 'occupied.' He's in love"

"Are you crushed out again? I told you not to do that. I told you to find someone who's actually straight to fixate on."

"It wouldn't fucking matter. What? Do you want me to go to the Whistle Stop or something? Try to pick up some lame bartender? I'm getting too old for that. I've gotten too old for this."

"Whatever. Just chill on the gay boys. 'Kay? Think attainability. And same for the straight girls."

"Right."

"But, God, oh, I didn't tell you! You remember Curtis right? From the Dustbin?"

"Oh no. Oh no. Oh no."

"No, Dylan's not hallucinating again. It's worse than that. Mel told me. Curtis was into some heavy shit for a while, you remember? He got into heroin a few years after you left. He'd been stringing it along for awhile. You know how him and Damian, they, he... he..."

"He's delicate, God..." The tears ran behind my eyes.

"He's susceptible to everything. He takes things hard. He's dead. He OD'd."

I set the phone down.

The red light blurred me out. Blurred me down. Moved me in to slug down the last dregs of my wine glass. Fold myself into the sheets.

I dreamt of Curtis. Perched on a windowsill. In my red-painted room. In Portland. Silver molding splayed around him. The walls streaked with collaged paintings of saints and angels. Smoking cigarettes in spiked collars. One wall had typewriter text about oranges. Next to Curtis, Marith was doubled up. Folded into herself. Her ballerina skirt billowed around pale arms spread flat to show the sharpie tattoos that he drew on her. They smiled. Giggling like children. A bottle of pink champagne half-visible on the floor.

Survivor's guilt. There comes a time when the death toll grows. When the people I've left behind come out. When I remember. Whether it's drugs. AIDS. Suicide. A random bullet in the night. It hurts that I go forwards and those I love sometimes do not. Why was I chosen to survive?

Is it actually a curse to survive with these memories. It was not a battle fought in the sense of a guns and ammo. My battle was fought along thighs. With coke straws. With long, endless nights. With empty bottles of whiskey. All the things I never said to you.

Curtis. Damian. Brady. Katie. I remember you. Micah, are you still out there somewhere? Facebook does not have all the answers.

I checked the Social Security death index periodically after I moved away from San Diego. I looked him up: Micah Pilar. There was no record of his death. I kept checking as the years passed. As his Facebook profile abruptly disappeared. As his phone was disconnected. As we lost touch. I hoped not to find what I feared. That he was dead.

2006. I fumbled with the lock on my mailbox. Hoped against hope that there might be mail today. The sun beat down on my sunburned shoulders. It was too hot to wear anything but a cotton halter from Express. I wiped sweaty hands on the black cotton. Popped open the mailbox. There was an envelope. A large envelope labeled CalArts!

I grabbed it. Sent a litter of Penny Saver newsprint to the pebble courtyard. Crouched down. Ripped it open. Saw the words, 'Welcome to the MFA Critical Studies Writing Program." I got into graduate school! A smile burst onto my face.

I sat on the Krakatoa patio. Sipping an iced coffee. With a long straw. Sheltered. By Magnolia trees and palms. Draped with Christmas lights. The patio extended in a circle. Around the small coffeehouse. Krakatoa was up the street from me.

I came to Krakatoa often. Always to sit alone. Read. Scratch in a notebook like a teenage virgin. Popping my characters to new postures. Bringing folders of the *Jet Set Desolate* manuscript to scribble and edit.

I saw a graying jaw that I thought was Micah. He was with a tall man. With sandy hair. Swim trunks. A prim-pawed Shih Tzu.

Timothy pulled out a chair. Set the dog in it neatly.

"Oh, hello, Lena," Tim said. "Meet Blanche."

Micah pulled out his own chair

"That's the baby's baby," he said.

"Oh, she's adorable."

"Oh, you have no idea." Micah scowled. "He flew the dog to Paris yet didn't take me. I feel like a coffee."

"No coffee today," said his boyfriend.

"Oh...."

"No."

I looked down. I knew that Timothy supported Micah. I knew equally well how insistent he could be. He asked me for money too.

"Well," Micah continued. "We went to Dos Flores last night for dinner. You would not believe what this man said to me! He said…"

"Oh, don't tell that story again," said Timothy. "We've heard it. We've done it We've been there. We've done that. I don't care that he didn't make your spring rolls extra minty like you asked, but..."

"I just wanted mint, and there was no mint. It's not too much to ask. It wasn't like I was having heart palpitations. It was just... It was just... It was like getting a mint julep with cilantro."

"Well tan my hide."

I giggled. The shade of the central palm dappled my forehead. Light and shade on the table. Slashes over the men's two ice waters. Like the undulations of a swimming pool in the dusk and twilight.

"So how have you been, dear?" Micah asked.

"I got the letter. I got into CalArts!"

"Oh you did? Oh my god, Timmy! This is kind of a big deal."

"Kind of? Oh most definitely! We are very proud of you, Lena."

I dimpled.

Micah began again. "Well in our world, the neighbor's been worse. We woke up on Thursday to him on the balcony. Holding a length of plastic tubing. Grimacing. In this particularly gruesome way."

"Heavens," I said.

"Oh yes, heavens! I was appalled! Simply appalled. We tried to call the police after he'd climbed back down again. They said they couldn't do anything. He didn't actually come in the house. A haunting! An apparition! We have a ghost. It's so not cute. He seemed threatening. Listen, Lena. He was yelling, 'I'll kill you! I'll fucking kill you!'"

"My God."

"Dreadful. Simply dreadful. I just don't know what we're going to do." Tim said.

"He's a paranoid Schizophrenic" added Micah, "I'm sorry. When doesn't take his meds he comes over here with a vengeance. He's opened my door in a full-on Mary Tyler Moore flip with lipstick smeared like blood across his face. I'm sorry, but if you're going to assault me, at least do good drag. Divine does not convince me, I want Candy Darling."

"Good luck." I said, "And I mean that."

Timothy left to feed the dog. Micah walked me home. On the corner in the alley between Krakatoa and Jarocco's the sun beat down. He took my hand.

"Morticia," he said. "Last night..." He brought my hand to his lips. "You screamed." He paused. "Like a banshee..." He kissed my wrist. "In a graveyard." Then up my arm. "By the light of the full moon." He folded my arm back. Mouthed my wrist. "Morticia, last night..." Another kiss. "You scared me." Again. "Morticia..."

I blushed.

"Do it again." He dropped my hand. Walked across the street. Micah was playing the bisexual triad game.

I fell backwards into a chain link fence. Two feral cats and a begonia marked my wake. I breathed. Watched him enter his gate. His boyfriend's dog, Blanche, frolicked on the scrabbled-dust grass outside with the cacti, to the spines. Lush grass fell inside the courtyard. The Sea World acrobats filled kiddie-pools and sat in them when the temperature reached 100.

I watched him walk away.

My Project Concern office desk was clean as Clorox-Wipes could make it. Indigenous Masai fabric wall hangings draped neatly behind my receptionist desk. The phone before me rang rarely. I was most often occupied with office supply orders. UPS shipments. To the nonprofit's outposts in Ethiopia. India. Nicaragua. Other parts of the world.

The job paid barely enough for gas to get there and back. A heartbreaking labor of love. Based on mutual exploitation. We both got to feel good about doing something good. With a little left over for wine, rent and tamales.

My boss and I had good working relationship. Sally was a sweet wide-eyed blonde who could motivate me to do pretty much anything.

I did a lot for Project Concern. I rewrote the employee manual. Revamped the filing system. I was the receptionist with the mostest. I tried as hard as I could. It was the last office job I ever had. I still failed. I always do.

I frenetically scribbled novel dialogue in my notebook. Under the desk. The new Executive Assistant came in. I trained her. Now she was my boss. Awkward.

My Ativan prescription wouldn't be renewable until next week. Dr. Montoya worried about the addictive potential of the stuff. I was made to sign all sorts of wavers and controlled substance disclosures before she would prescribe it the first time. My County Mental Health Doctor urged me to consider stopping the anti-anxiety treatment now that we were three weeks past the break-in. She said I should have found my peace by now.

"You lost a TV. You lost a blender. It's just stuff." I clutched my cell phone to my ear in the work bathroom. Hoped no one was in the stalls. I told my doctor that my old housemate in Portland died. My best friend in San Diego was HIV+. I was worried about grad school.

My psychiatrist agreed to write me another prescription, but only one. Then I would transfer doctors to someone in Valencia. Someone near CalArts. Then it would be out of her hands. One week to go. One week before I could get my Ativan. My Lorazepam. I loved the long, languorous generic name. I loved writing long, languorous dialogue for my heroine in my notebook to be typed up when I got home.

I was anxious without Lorazepam,

My new boss did not love that I wrote a novel at work. She also did not love the fact that I took eight sick days. In the last two months. To see my psychiatrist.

At the dinner table, my mother told me. Over and over. I should lie to Project Concern. About going to graduate school. So that they would hire me. Then I could actually see a real psychiatrist. Get more regular therapy. A therapist that could work on that escalating alcoholism.

All I ever wanted was to be safe. Secure. Have enough to eat. Something to do that felt good. Health care.

I lied about so many things to keep jobs. Keep having enough to eat. I never told any employer that I was a Bipolar drug addict.

However, lying about that one thing that I was so desperately proud of? That I was going to remake myself? Go to the hallowed halls of California Institute of the Arts? Be legitimized? Redeemed? That I would not lie about. I had that sliver of pride left. So Project Concern knew that I was leaving for graduate school in three weeks. I told them.

I had a panic attack. Left abruptly after lunch. Jenni fired me. Right then and there.

I stared out at the rooftops. From my lounge on Micah's bed. The expanse swathed with cowboy sheets. Bloodstains. Two weeks had passed since I was fired. Timothy out of town. I was over at Micah's. I was about to leave Golden Hill forever.

The French doors opened onto the summer night. The sky luminescent with stars. Over palm trees. Bursting to the skyline. Micah smoked a cigarette out the balcony. Stared fiercely into the night. His arms were marred with bandages. His jaw clenched. The fairy-wisps of smoke drifted up along the tall green stripes. On the walls surrounding.

The bang came suddenly. Like artillery downstairs with a guttural roar behind. I took a long drink of the Shiraz on the bedside table.

Band-Aids. Dior Pour Homme. The roar came again with the sound of breaking glass.

I ran a hand across my short, bleached hair. Smoothed it over the two cowboys on the sheets traipsing around a campfire in lockstep. The bed Micah shared with his boyfriend.

Micah spoke, "There's nothing we can do."

"Are you sure? Can't we call the police?"

"I've tried. They tell me that as long as he doesn't actually come into the apartment, there's nothing that they can do."

"Good lord." I took another drink. My lips stained purple.

I curled up into a ball on the bed. Cupped my knees. The ceiling fan turned and turned above us. Beads of moisture formed on the blades.

Micah got up in his boxers. Tossed the Camel out the window. Stalked into the bathroom. A huge wooden carousel rooster stood guard along the wall. Orange beak curved to steal, to bite.

My bare legs stretched behind me in shirt and panties only, I turned away. Waited. I was good at waiting.

It was too hot to wear clothes. We had crept out of our clothes slowly with the wine. The daytime heat not abated with the night's advancing. Timothy was away. Working. Painting ceilings in anther country.

There was a wrenching sound from below. I cringed. A yell. I yelped. Skittered off the bed towards the stairs. Up or down, there was no relief. Only upwards. Outwards. Towards the sky to fly. Over the narrow courtyard with its row of kiddy pools. Cacti. To the spines.

Micah emerged in his bedroom.

"Look, he said, "I don't know. I don't know anywhere else I can go. I know you can go home. You should. There's no need to stay here with me."

I stared up at him. Shredded the sheets beneath my fingers. Knew this was his boyfriend's apartment. Not my own. It was wrong for me to lay half-naked in his bed. Stay past the designated hour. I lingered.

I linger still.

I was just so attracted to Micah. My dashing bisexual friend. I was so alone in the world. I knew that whatever I gave him, sexually, would not matter at this point. I was about to leave town.

"No, I can't."

"I wouldn't be mad. You can."

"I won't."

"Then let's dance." He turned to the record player. Put on a Johnny Mathis record. "Twelfth of Never" came on. Micah reached out to me.

"Come."

I rose. Let him wrap me in a waltz. Ballroom dancing to records was something Micah and I did together. Part of our pantomime of romance. I fumbled in my steps as his broad arms wrapped my waist. A rattle and a shriek came from downstairs.

"Don't think," said Micah. He twirled me. I stepped free. Wrapped back into his arms as he flicked his wrist. We were practiced. Just as practiced at turning away.

I fell to kiss his neck.

"That's entirely enough of that." Micah smiled softly. Let me go.

His shoulder bandage fell. It was a drunken mirror accident: Vicodin. Red wine. He crushed his way into his boyfriend's floor-length mirror. This earned him a substantial phone lecture. Earlier that weekend. From Timothy.

I stared at his arms. From the other side of the bed. He talked on the phone that afternoon. My finger traced forwards. From time to time. Withdrew again. Extended with longing. Clamped around the sheet.

Micah had to know that I wanted him. Was it just that he was so financially dependent on his boyfriend? Perhaps. I tried.

There was blood all over the sheets now from Micah's wound. Dried blood. I knew it was HIV+ infected blood but I didn't care. I rolled around in it. Sprawling. My legs tunneling through the sheets.

I kissed Micah's neck again.

"No, Lena, I can't. I really can't."

"But – "

"It's more than just Tim. It's the fact that you're about to leave forever. I don't want my parting present to you to be *that.* My HIV. You know this. Even with a condom, there is risk."

"I know."

"No. For the last time, no." I stared down at my hands. Micah walked again to the window. Stared out fiercely. What I would have done for him.

Micah reached for his cigarettes. Pulled one out slowly.

"It's a warm night," he said.

I put my clothes back on. Gathered my things.

Downstairs, there was the sound of breaking glass.

Chapter 5 — MFA FIRST YEAR

Fall of 2006. I did the paperwork. Took out student loans. Enrolled at CalArts for an MFA in Critical Studies. I had a new life in Valencia. A wealthy desert suburb. Thirty miles north of Los Angeles.

I moved into the graduate dorms. Struck how tiny and Spartan the rooms were. A burlap wall. A twin single bed. A blue plastic wrapped mattress. A blonde wood desk. A deep, uncomfortable chair. I filled my room with paintings I was able to save from Portland and San Francisco. A red Ikea lamp illuminated many a drunken sexual conquest.

I lived on campus. In a tiny, eight by eight foot burlap-walled dorm room. Stuffed with paintings and curios. Subsistence living conditions all over again,

I was back in college. For the first time since 1998. For that first year, I lived in this bacchanalian promiscuity. Went to readings for the first time. Art openings. Theatre performances. Parties. Concerts. Trysts by night. Drunk on red wine. Carrying my flask full of Smirnoff.

I partied a lot at CalArts. I met a lot of amazing people going to art openings on campus. Every Thursday night, there was a series of galleries showing in the main building. With cheap wine and student art shows. They were a perfect social event. It was college all over again. I was finally getting laid. All over again. After a year and a half of unwilling celibacy in San Diego.

October 2006, I turned thirty. In a Silver Lake bar called Cha Cha Cha. My two dorm mates sat with me at the small table.

Anne was only my friend in that dorm right in the beginning. We bonded by talking about acting in the dorm kitchen. While I nursed glasses of wine. I went to the theatre a lot as a child. Respected actors. Anne didn't like to drink.

Neither did Animation MFA Shimbe. His Korean name was Beum Sik Shim. He was tall and brilliant. A lanky animator. I noticed him immediately on moving in. We met waiting together in the long orientation lines. Briefly, momentarily dated. He broke up with me after the first two weeks. He was just too busy with schoolwork. Didn't have any time for a girlfriend. I understood.

When I got to CalArts, I felt a dim panic in my chest. I had to take advantage of the student health insurance. Assure what I felt I already knew.

I envisioned my tragic death of AIDS. The hoped-for posthumous publication of my book. My possible canonization: as a Rimbaud for our times. Who lived and died as boldly and ephemerally as shattered vacuum tubes. So I liked to imagine myself. What was I thinking? I was too old. Ridiculous, embarrassing fantasies foundered in my mind. Coping. With the grim reality. Of my chronic illness.

I went to the on-campus health clinic. In the main CalArts building. My second day there. The nurse slid the needle into my arm. I saw the plume of blood wend upward for the HIV test.

A week passed. A week passed where I slid my fingers through my new boyfriend's hair. Tried not to think of what I would tell him.

A week passed. I tromped through the halls to the cafeteria.

"Would I quit school if I was HIV+?" I thought? No, school was all I had. I couldn't go back to the knife-needle-grills of San Francisco. There was no choice but to go on. Take the meds if that was what it came to.

I waited for my results. Nothing. Anxious moments flooding their way through classes. Writing. Sleep. A week passed.

8:45 am. I crept through the Heath Services door. Tugged at the sleeve of the bemused adjunct doctor. He pulled on his latex gloves. Giggled with the nurse.

"Hey, can I get my results?"

The doctor seemed amused by my urgency. My shaking hands. My assurance that the last remainder of my life would be blared vivid in the next ten seconds.

"You're fine" he said." You're negative."

"You mean I – "

"Of course. Come on. You're not going to get AIDS. You're a grad student."

Yeah, and that only happens to junkies and homosexuals. Right. And homeless people. The disposable people.

Right.

I limped out of there in my boots with a tromp that felt unsure. Not even sure how to navigate without my noble death scenario. My artist-as-tragic-hero mythos that I so carefully nurtured for the last week. It gave me the will to endure my terror of my colleagues. Terror of offending a teacher. Terror of turning in an inappropriate or somehow uncouth text that would reveal me as unacademic. Disgusting. Fully unable to handle this rarified environment that I had somehow tricked my way into.

I was going to live. I had to learn how to live.

I was at a David Wojnarowicz film screening. In Hollywood. With a friend. AIDS in art came up again. The dire condition. Refracted with the initial drive. To canonize. Romanticize. Decry. Cast it aside for the next "now" cause.

We sat on folding chairs. A strikingly beautiful woman. In a filmy brown blouse. Read about the emotive qualities of Wojnarowicz's work.

His films forced the viewer to experience the disease. We sat behind professors.

I sat next to a girl in my MFA program. A girl with an un-locatable European accent. Short Truffaut-esque hair. I did not know her. I was afraid to speak to her.

We watched. Grainy ants swarmed over crucifixes. Cocks penetrated. Fled. Wojnarowicz's voice again and again recited the litany of his pain. The eighties governmental blind eye to the disease, His own vow to still experience his own sexuality and the beauty of queer men despite his designation as a walking infection. The virulent and vicious bearer of death.

We filed out.

I heard the girl with the Truffaut hair say in clipped tones, "AIDS? It's just so dated. I was bored."

I wanted to punch her in the face. Amid the plastic glasses of white wine. The collage-decoupage paintings on the walls. I wanted to watch her tumble backwards into Chris Kraus. Her glass of two-buck-chuck Merlot tumbling scarlet against her rabbit fur jacket. I wanted to see her fall.

Micah may still be alive. I don't know, anymore. Thirty-five is not enough. Forty-five is not enough. Eighty-five is enough. Ninety-five is enough.

I wanted a *Valley of the Dolls* party. With Micah there. Someday.

Micah drifted away. Away with time. As I drift from all of the people I write about. People I have known. Who touched my life.

This is for you.

My own desire. To memorialize. Preserve tragedy. It troubled me. *Rent* memorialized Jonathon Larson. I wanted to memorialize my friends and lovers. I did not trust this urge.

Writing *Jet Set Desolate,* In San Francisco, I was close to Brady. Wanted to freeze his effervescent beauty in time. I wanted to place him on Amazon. To be experienced. By that odd soul. Who might pick up my book. Somehow make him last. Longer than his life. Could promise him.

Another grandiose fantasy. I was into those. They took the edge off the addictive-bipolar self-loathing. Gin and ginger took the edge off my loves. Off dictating their real names. Taking once again their stories. Laying them out. For a high pass. To a CalArts professor. Give them the bleeding edge.

Whore out the truth. Validation.

First semester. Narrative Ethics. With Jon Wagner. I wrote an essay. About my relationship. With AIDS.

They workshopped my AIDS essay. I cried.

"This is an ethical disaster. I have to ask, is she serious?" Jon Wagner said in workshop. HIs reddened hands on the table. My humiliation.

I sent Wagner a regretful email. Dropped the class. Now everyone in my program knew just how dirty. Ridiculous. I was. Shame. Shame was routine. I bared my soul. Was condemned. In alchemy. The crucible. Of graduate school.

At CalArts. I didn't talk to Micah. For months. I yearned. To talk to him.

Finally, Micah called me. We spoke briefly.

"Keep in touch." Micah said. I didn't tell him what I was writing.

The calls faded away.

I still don't know if Micah reads my work. It comforts me to hope he's alive. Out there.

My attenuated writer antennae were drawn towards "the story." Yearning towards the juicy anecdote. The vignette. The gossip. The scraps of narrative. that I spouted to a friend in a bar. Between classes. Over burritos. At Las Delicias.

HIV became a source of inspiration. Exploitation. I took it up. I took it up again and again.

I wrote about AIDS. Made my friends into characters. Tried to merge them into the same character.

I churned forth the same material. Analyzed the convergence of death sentences as a narrative function of continuity. The dispassionate logic of literary assemblage seemed so trivializing.

I distrusted the very nature of writing when I was in a graduate program for it. Stealing lives? Refashioning narratives from scraps and skits? Professors said what I did was wrong. Bad writing.

Is it that way? Again? With each book or essay that I write? Can I afford to care? No. I preserve people's stories. Forever. The writing. I am born to do. Writing is more important than people. I do what I have to do.

All my life, I have been irrevocably wedded. To the process. The mechanism. Of confessional writing. Developing. Detachment. From the rawness. Of horrifying material. To the logical demands. Of the narrative continuum. This is how my writing works. This is what has to be done. Published. To turn trauma out.

I have to go on. Survivor's guilt. Narrative ethics.

If my subjects are uncomfortable with their actions represented in text? Is it their problem, not mine? If they don't like it? For not understanding what writer's do?

Perhaps? Writing about people I know. Is fine. If the ethical transgressions in my work angered people? I can't afford to care.

Writing is more important than people. I can't stop writing anymore.

"Silence = Death," The AIDS activists chant.

2007. CalArts. I write on my Dell desktop computer. In a black notebook. At the campus coffeeshop.

I remember Brady. In his parlor. In San Francisco. When we lived together. Stubble. Long legs. In fiercely tight pants. Brady told me another friend wrote about him. In a novel. Using his real name. Brady said, "In my friend's book, he said: 'Brady in the hospital. Shitting his pants. In bed. The nurse wouldn't allow him to use the toilet. Said he would 'infect the children.'"

I listened that night. In San Francisco. To how another writer coped with Brady's illness. Tried to be more ethical in my own work. Wondered, with shame, if I was.

It hurt me. To hear Brady tell. He felt exploited by another writer. It hurt me. That my friend. Who seemed so noble. Would be so pained. It hurt me. To realize the dangers of representation.

Pain. Despite the necessity of authorization. Gorgeous transgression of the told. Honesty. T of danger. The sold-out soul of the subject.

For it was the subject who hurt in the end. Not the author. I'm fine.

Brady told me in San Francisco before he died that he wanted me to write about him. Brady wanted me to write *Jet Set Desolate* to memorialize him. He wanted to be heroic.

How it hurt me to kill him in the end of the book. Brady spilled his blood in blue rose bruises beneath the hands of my stock abusive boyfriend. I had to face up to the death of my friend. It was a visceral, real and possible death.

Subtle webs of delusion in which I comforted my writing mind. I loved Brady. I loved Micah. I made out with Curtis in spin the bottle games in Portland. The death toll grew.

I thought of Micah. He called me from South Carolina. Applied for schools. Worked in a hotel. Left his boyfriend. Rented an apartment. Dancing fabulously against the strictures of disability and depression. Enacting his personal strength against the limitations of his body. His psycho-chemical imbalances.

I had to go on. It was never that simple.

I met my CalArts first year BFF at an orientation mixer in the campus coffee shop. She came up to me. Said that she recognized me from Reed. I got my undergraduate degree there. In Portland. I didn't remember this effervescent girl. She said we had had a writing class together. With Rick Hillis. My first writing professor.

We talked. Sipped our coffee.

I learned that Rachel recently married. Was taking time away from her professor husband in San Diego to get an MFA in Costume Design at CalArts. She worked and lived with her husband Aaron for seven years through his PhD. Now he was teaching in San Diego.

Aaron and Rachel met at Reed. College sweethearts. Neither who I remembered but both of whom remembered me.

I was popular at Reed. River once referred to Reed as my Warhol years.

Rachel and I were instant friends.

I had a car on campus. The grey-blue Oldsmobile Cutlass Ciera that my grandmother gave me when she went into the rest home. Rachel and I made plans to go see a production of Marat/Sade that was playing in LA at a small theatre called Sacred Fools.

Rachel and I had an intense, short friendship. We were utter and total BFFs my first MFA year and the following summer. Fall 2006 to Fall 2007.

My BF and I took pilgrimages to the MAC counters in the Valley. Had bikini time. Tanned at the CalArts pool. Drank vodka from flasks while working in the costume design/set design lab. We would share a big double bottle of Yellowtail Cabernet-Merlot in my dorm room every night. Talk out everything that bothered us.

We never slept together because she was married, although I would have. I came on to her once. She turned me down saying something about boundaries. She was right, but I didn't know it yet. I just loved her so completely the way I always love my sweet transitory best friends.

I sever with another best friend and I am heartbroken for a time once more. Every relationship has a lifetime. Best friends, boyfriends and girlfriends have lifetimes. Unfortunately, so did my wife. Unfortunately, so do I.

The first year, Rachel and I drank wine with her husband. He drove up from San Diego on the weekends. Rachel's apartment was down the street from CalArts in Valencia. Had a pool. Hot tub. Cool white carpeting.

Rachel's roommate for the first part of that year wouldn't let any of us drink in their two-bedroom apartment. He was sober. Rachel thought the dry house was okay at first when she first moved in. When she met me, she realized she wanted to drink with me. So Rachel and her husband would take me out to dinner. Come over to my dorm room afterwards to drink.

Many CalArts students came over to my dorm room that first year. 2006-2007. The alcohol was always flowing. My dorm room was the place to drink. We talked into late in the night about art dreams.

Rachel and Aaron drove me into Los Angeles for delicious dinners. Aaron was a foodie. They were generous about buying me dinner. I never reciprocated. Probably this failure eventually doomed our social triad. I just couldn't afford to pay for dinner on my meagre student loan budget. Aaron came from money and had a good professor job. I came from money too but my parents weren't giving me any yet.

I let these friends deep into my life that first year. It was my first experience being friends with a happily married couple.

Rachel and I were only BFFs for a year. But for a year, it was glorious. We would meet every evening in my dorm room to split a big bottle of Yellowtail Cabernet-Merlot. Talk about everything.

On Thursdays we dressed up. Filled big gulp cups with red wine. Walked around the big main building on campus going to art openings. Met artists who became famous later. In my case, hooking up with said artists.

My vivacious friend was the perfect wingman. She liked to call herself a "married cougar." Flash her big wedding ring at all the men who tried to hit on her.

On the weekends when all of the LA people were away, it was quiet on campus. Rachel and I stayed in her apartment complex hot tub with glasses of wine. I loved my new life in Santa Clarita.

Chapter 6 — ART SCHOOL CONFIDENTIAL

I scribbled through writing workshops. Film classes. Art classes. Tutored ESL students in various subjects my first year. A part-time job that I was woefully unprepared for. I hadn't studied whatever obscure art discipline my students were studying. I didn't speak their language. I was really only useful to my BFA tutees as language practice. I was happy to oblige English language conversation. If I could get my hung over ass out of bed. Some of my ESL students found a new tutor. I didn't blame them.

A back problem in early in the first year had me visiting a chiropractor. He told me to throw out my mattress and get a new one. I got rid of my plastic-lined dorm mattress. Was unable to afford a new one. I slept on wood slats. Towels. Blanket piles. Slept on rolled up coats for the rest of the year. No wonder guys never stayed over. My bed was incredibly uncomfortable. I had to be blind drunk to fall asleep on it. I usually was.

My lack of a proper mattress prompted my friend Marsian DeLellis to ask, "Don't your parents love you?" Marsian was a wealthy puppetry MFA who only ate things from Whole Foods.

Whether or not my parents loved me, they definitely weren't going to give me any more money. I discovered that the second semester.

I crashed my car.

I left Rachel's one evening after dinner. Drove the thirty miles into Los Angeles to meet up with Sarah. She wasn't at her little Highland Park house yet.

While I waited for Sarah in my car, Ian from *Jet Set Desolate* texted me. He lived in Venice now. Ran a graphic design firm. Recently got a DUI, so needed me to pick him up.

Naively, I drove all the way to Venice that night. Picked Ian up. I still believed then that there was hope for Ian and I. To rekindle what we had in San Francisco.I drove back from Venice with Ian in the passenger seat. On a freeway onramp the brakes in my old car went out. I couldn't stop the car. Turned head-on into oncoming traffic.

I ran the car into a tree, to finally stop it. Terrifying.

We got out of my wrecked Oldsmobile, Ian helped me get a tow-truck to his cottage in Venice. I slept with him that night. The next morning, Ia rode the bus with me into Santa Monica. I rented a car. Drove back to CalArts. We never spoke again.

After I crashed my car I ran out of financial aid money. Couldn't get another mattress. I had to endure the hardness of my bed.

I went hungry second semester of my first year. Wasted away to bones. I had class from four pm to seven pm three days a week. The CalArts cafeteria that held all of my Board Points stopped serving at seven pm. I missed all the food. With no car or money the second semester of the first year, I had trouble feeding myself.

I stole rice from Shimbe's rice cooker. Stole my dorm-mate Anne's frozen Italian dinners from the freezer. Anne knew I was taking her food. She later refused any Facebook friendship post-CalArts. I burned that bridge by stealing her Michelina's microwave lasagna.

I went to karaoke in the dismal local townie bar with Anne and the other actors a couple of times. Left to meet up with Rachel to drink red wine and gossip. When Rachel quit drinking in 2007? We much quit being friends. When she was drinking together, we were best drinking buddies.

My other drinking buddies began to materialize around campus. A muscular ex-boxer and another fellow in my writing program.

Fall, 2006. I sat down with a cup of coffee. Considered the computer screen. i had to write a short story. To flirt with postmodern strategies. Array a token set of impersonal tropes.

Writing felt difficult in my current state. I was ill-suited to the practice when hung over. I looked at the screen again. Was it at all appropriate to mention my romantic ills? My current inability to do anything but curl under blankets? Plugged into my new iPod. To write about my psychiatric disabilities? I tried. I couldn't yet.

Chapter 7 — VALLEY OF THE DOLLS REDUX

My dorm mate and I sat in the squalid dorm kitchen. On the paltry hard couches. Our complaints about the limited hours and bizarre, bureaucratic obfuscations of CalArts administrators multiplied.

Anne rose from the couch. Got back to rehearsal.

I turned back to *Valley of the Dolls*. Anne Welles put on her Gilmore Girl face. Went to lunch with Lyon Burke. Her paramour who just arrived back from WWII. Lyon wanted to write a novel. So did I.

I read *Valley of the Dolls* over and over when I should have been reading *Naked Lunch*.

"I read an article once..." Siouxsie and the Banshee's "Ninety-Two Degrees" begins with this phrase. "I read an article once that said more murders are committed at 92 degrees then many other temperature...It's just 92, people get irritable."

No. No. The article I read said that 81% of all Americans believe they have a novel in them and only a minute percentage actually do the work of writing the novel. No one wants to actually sit down and write that book. The article cited this. Mainly that people just wanted to publish one. Get famous, as happens to so few writers.

I wanted literary fame so badly that I could taste it. Ever elusive.

When I was in San Francisco, drifting around in nightclubs with feathers in my hair, I heard a lot of young men say that they could write a novel. They just had to sit down and do it. I would take them home with me. Show them *Jet Set Desolate*. See what they thought.

Some said, "Slapstick sex farce. Does this get deeper?" Some decided I was Anais Nin. Score.

Fundamentally it was the lonely writer's pathetic plea for validation. I'm still that way. If you read me I'm thrilled.

Look at me! I do something! It is valuable even though nobody understands it. I wrote in complete isolation in San Francisco and San Diego. I believed no-one would ever publish me beyond Internet porn.

Writing was a pathetic plea for validation. Still.

"Did you read my story? What did you think?" I asked my classmates.

I was constantly consumed by the idea that no-one would take me seriously.

I got my start writing for the Internet with porn. I had never taught before. Unlike my peers. I was the worst ESL tutor ever. Had two unpublishable, transgressive novels put away. I felt like a crank. A fraud in the house of art school.

I feared academia. These ditz moments caught me. Apologetic. Self-conscious. Amid my more serious peers. I couldn't keep my scandals secret. I had a big mouth. Wild hands on the keyboard spilling secrets.

My yearning for connection was so impossible. So apart. That yearning blanched me out. From intangible passion? To the crushing entirety of defeat. Of denial. Of solitude.

2007. I was thirty. Living in a dorm. Single. Getting older. I watched my DVD of *Valley of the Dolls* over and over. Memorized the dialogue.

A stream of lovers on that hard dorm bed.

My CalArts class came together that first year to make a now-lost student B-film. I played several prostitutes and a gypsy. The roles I was given felt appropriate. I hid my embarrassment. Camped it up in a red silk kimono. Unlit opium pipe. Most of my lines were cut from the final cut of the film. I didn't enunciate. I hid my humiliation at the screening. Didn't push for my colleagues to put me on the film screening flyer. I knew my bits mostly ended up on the cutting room floor.

I took Lorazepam daily. The County Mental Health psychiatrist kept prescribing it.

Ego is a function of the artist. Whether the primordially feminine ego of the actress. Model. Writer who labors in neurotic obscurity. There was that fundamental drive to be noticed for something.

I remember childhood art classes Actually having the yarn and popsicle stick God's Eye that everyone liked the best. Even though my eyes were not watching God. Nor he I. I could understand that joy. Sought it still in my graduate school classes. It pained me when I did not succeed.

The Critical Studies program was very competitive. There were twenty of us in each class. The degree took two years. We all knew that when we got out we would be desperately competing for the agents, publications, teaching jobs and book deals that only a few of us would get. The calculated gamble of all of the student loans most of us took out. In hopes of a later advance from a publisher that would would the debt away.

Striving against my mind's limitations. I apologized for my crass ineptitude all the time. I was overcome by *Valley of the Dolls*. Returned to the text. Kept writing.

CalArts was contained in one sprawling air-conditioned building. Warrens of corridors. It took me a long time to figure out the building. Find my classes.

One night, Rachel and I browsed the art openings. I met a handsome gay man with a moustache. The three of us got stuck in an elevator together. A man with dreadlocks played upright bass. Inside the golden wood elevator leading to the Provost's office.

Omar and I talked. The elevator went up and down. Thumps of bass. We kept drinking. Talking. When we finally left the elevator, Omar and I were friends.

Omar and I ran all around campus that night. Went back to my dorm. We never slept together. He was gay. I accepted that early on. After the lessons of Micah and Brady. Omar was Pakistani. Recently out of a long-term relationship with an older man, who took him briefly to New York. They co-parented an elegant Italian Greyhound.

Omar lived in a brightly hued studio in North Hollywood. He drove carless me over there to to hang out. We stayed up all night doing his Adderall. Talking. Drawing each other. He was a BFA in Set Design. Recently transferred from Otis's Toy Design program. He had a desk in the set design lab. I ran into him there. We would drink coffee. Get fast food. Talk all night. Go to gay bars and parties in the city. Omar introduced me to Akbar, the only gay bar left in Silver Lake. We stayed up late taking his Adderall. Walking up and down the winding halls.

Omar was the perfect accomplice. We stalked CalArts campus for many long, insomniac nights. He smoked cigarettes. Worked on foam core set models in the design studio. I read. Or wrote. Swigging straight vodka from my flask. Omar's Adderall allowed me to read one book after another, as I needed to do. High on what was still essentially pharmaceutical meth, I saw fairies in the wood grain. I believed in fairies.

CalArts was a magical place. Walt Disney's cryogenically frozen head was rumored to be stored in the sub-level. I believed it.

The sub-level was the lowest level to sprawling central building. It held artist studios and a few classrooms, including the one I TA'd in the second year. It was covered with layer upon layer of the most creative graffiti. Graffiti like urban lichen traces of so many students over the years.

Confessional writing was frowned upon at CalArts. My professors and my more favored peers were all about experimental writing. I could appreciate experimental writing sometimes. I just couldn't do it.

Sometimes, I couldn't even understand experimental writing. I just endured it. My eyes skimmed over the assigned page. I knew Kenneth Goldsmith wrote books he didn't actually expect anyone to read. Just having Goldsmith books on the coffee table made one seem academic and literary. Did people actually read them?

I stared at the blank page. How to play with language? To observe the ciphers on the page like the ants that crawled across the table in my dormitory kitchen.

In the kitchen, Shim dithered. He closed a notebook.

"Do you have any time tonight?" He asked. "There's this experimental animation showcase. They're showing my film. Do you want to go?" I limped against the side of the refrigerator. Held an espresso machine cartridge full of damp coffee grounds.

"Yes, I'll go," I said without looking at him.

Back to my homework. To fall back into the trenches of traditional narrative realism. That was the enemy and the mother. Everything I'd ever written before in San Francisco and San Diego was suddenly suspect. Now unwelcome with the new aesthetics I was learning.

My fingers clenched above the keyboard. A long stare at the orange wood of the desk. At the stapler's oblique angle. At the mug with a Grecian design of New York coffee cups. A gift from another man who disappointed me.

This terminology was really going to have to go if I was going to get experimental, I urged myself. I could not say my heart was broken. All personalities depicted must be satiric. Must be distant. Must be removed from the sad and tedious drivel of my daily life. To be painfully earnest and honest as I am was frowned upon.

Girl met boy in small Southern California art school. Fleeting month of bliss ensued. Boy dismissed girl due to overwhelming homework pressures. Various unknown, imagined, poorly communicated reasons that he found it difficult to articulate with his still-limited English.

Shimbe came to CalArts directly from South Korea. He fed me Kim Chi and rice. I fed him chicken and *South Beach Diet* spaghetti squash cooked in the dorm kitchen.

"Did you break up with me because I didn't want children?" I wanted to ask Shimbe. He wouldn't be the first man to reject me for this choice.

All of my love life woes had to be be put to the side if the academic, appropriate, experimental, and drivingly suitable story of self-conscious flippancy I wanted to write for class was ever going to happen. My over-arching drive was to be literary.

Was there even literary fiction anymore? Did people read it? I didn't know.

Was there a place for me? I didn't know. I was lost in the hall of academic mirrors like a Sleeping Beauty snow globe. Lost all perspective.

I wrote in a letter to an agent in 2006 saying that *Jet Set Desolate* was literary fiction. The agent asked for a full manuscript. Marked it up. Rejected it. Said my sentences were tortured. They were. The manuscript was too short. A novella. I was enamored of commas and semicolons. I didn't realize that the period is the most devastating punctuation mark.

I wasn't done revising *Jet Set Desolate*. I wrote to set the pain down. Keep a record. Set trauma down so I never had to think about it. Genre fiction was suspect. Especially the confessional. Mystery, sci-fi and fantasy were anathema at art school. Each student had their angle. So did I. Dissolute, pornographic autobiographical fantasy.

My computer's spell-check never understood the word "transgressive." The word "problematize." This became increasingly problematic. I tried to sound as academic as my education allowed. I was in over my head. Again,

"No, no. It's not me and you. Watch the POV," I told myself.

In 1998, an undergraduate professor told me I hadn't lived enough. Not enough to have good material. He told me to graduate from Reed. Go out to live. Gather material. I took eight years off to do all of the drugs. Was that what he meant? I'll never know.

Writing about heartbreak reflected my own mundanity. A rising sense of guilt for work undone. Necessary. Never enough coffee. I read if couldn't write. Several classes assigned us a book a week. I set down the notebook. Turned to read *Naked Lunch* for Textual Strategies.

In the end I listened to the *Valley of the Dolls* record over and over. I had the record cover pinned to my dorm room wall. Hid the book away with the *Harry Potter* and *The Chronicles of Narnia. In* box under my bed. Far away from the Genet, Debord, Kristeva and Cortazar on my display bookshelves.

Why were these writers whom I felt comfortable publicly liking mostly men? Except the token one whose soul cause was femininity? Kristeva writing about the female orgasm of jouissance? Jaqueline Susann fed my occasional quest for light reading. Susann fed me more then even Debord.

My back clenched over the keyboard. I nibbled cafeteria peanuts. I waited in anger for the campus coffeeshop to open when it was clearly ten am. All I wanted was another cup of coffee.

The pink boudoirs of New York ingénues held only fleeting charm. *Valley of the Dolls* had dubious literary value,

I expelled myself. I spit myself out. I became abject. With the same motion through which I tried to become established. Amid the violence of sobs and vomit at CalArts, I was reborn an artist. In self-destructive jouissance. The little death of Bataille. Thanatos. The death-drive to annihilate. To explode into "Forget Domani," as Frank Sinatra sang.

I couldn't do drugs anymore. I couldn't if I wanted to have a future. I had to go on.

Chapter 7 – DIFFERENT HOLLYWOODS

I was reading a lot. Several books per week. Writing short stories. Academic essays unlike the personal essays I wrote prolifically for the Internet from 2012 onward. When confessional writing finally had its moment. I revised my two books *Jet Set Desolate* and *Neon Hysteric* that I wrote in San Francisco and San Diego. Combined them on Matias' suggestion to become *Jet Set Desolate.* My CalArts thesis. My first novel.

I worked hard on my craft then in the evenings: wine. Wine and Rachel. I suppose I was in love with her as I always am with my BFF.

Rachel was falling in love with a CalArts filmmaker. Drifting away from her husband as their marriage soured with distance. I watched their divorce entropy slowly with fascination as I later watched *Mad Men* and other married friend's divorce entropy.

Marriage always seemed to end in divorce. After the catastrophic failure of being widowed by my first marriage in 2012 I resolved never to try marriage again.

I dated a super-talented black MFA actress named Diona Reasonover for a few weeks in 2007. Diona was funny and cool. A comic actor. I liked her a lot. I gave her head in a sublevel alcove the first time we hooked up.

Diona kept thinking I said racist things when I was drunk, or things she interpreted as racist. I didn't want to be racist at all. I was just really drunk all the time. That's no excuse.

My girlfriend Diona and I didn't work out for social reasons. mostly. A disagreement over whether we would go to my writing program holiday party together at the last minute. Diona wanted to go with her actor friend with the long braids to see "The Women" performed with midgets. She went to the play instead of my party.

It was so important to me to show the classmates I had been so promiscuous with that I finally had a girlfriend. Diona just wasn't that interested in being shown off. I broke up with Diona for not backing me up and doing my activity. It was petty.

Diona got another girlfriend pretty quickly. They seemed pretty solid and happy for the rest of CalArts. I observed her from a distance.

In 2016 Diona is a famous actress on television. She has a different girlfriend and a new exuberant weave. I saw it all on Facebook. I still observe her from a distance as I do all my exes. I drove past a billboard of Diona's face on the Sunset Strip when I was going to the Standard Hotel in 2015 with my poetry book publisher.

I watched Diona's Saturday Night Live audition reel on YouTube one lonely night years later. It blew my mind. So fucking talented.

Rachel and I got very into bikini time, as we called it in 2006-2007. Tanning. Done at her pool at her apartment complex or the campus pool. The campus pool was lush and lovely in the middle of the BFA dorm. I would swim there in my new green bikini. My fingers parting the waves.

I began to wear the wedding ring from my first engagement on my right hand. A tiny diamond in a simple setting. Influenced by my BFF Rachel's diamond wedding ring. She encouraged me to appropriate my old wedding ring as a right hand ring. Right hand rings were seen as a sign of female empowerment then, at least to me. I didn't have a husband or wife yet to give me the much-coveted diamonds Rachel had.

I wrote in *Jet Set Desolate* about my prior engagement to Jesse in San Francisco. He did me wrong. It felt right to wear the ring again. To reclaim my failed engagement. My grandma Janet in the rest home originally gave me that ring, not Jesse.

My junkie ex-boyfriend didn't even supply the ring when we got engaged. I should have known something was wrong right there. Big red flag.

I had a bracelet made of typewriter keys that I wore every day. A gift from my mother at Christmas. I dressed with the mad abandon of art school. Cutting and re-sewing T-shirts to new combinations. My hair curled black cautiously past my shoulders. Curling from all the medication I was on. On my lips I wore MAC red liquid lip stain that I brushed on in the Butler building bathroom with the tiny brush every day. Let it dry into a cracking sheen that proclaimed my ruthlessness.

I was in it to win it. But I almost lost it all.

Ants roamed the bare bones California dorms. People didn't sleep over too often. But they did come over for sex. I was mostly single and playing the field the first year, except for the three weeks or so dating Diona. I marked flings with Dante and Daniel from my writing program. Sex was casual again. Fun.

I didn't tell anyone about my herpes or HPV. I was too scared of rejection. I always used condoms although I had a Nuva Ring. I was too scared of becoming a pariah in my tenuous new community. I lived in fear yet lulled myself with wine.

I let people find out about the herpes in 2009 when I had just left CalArts by leaving that squalid factoid buried at the climax of *Jet Set Desolate*. My first year mentor Janet Sarbanes said a pregnancy scare didn't have high enough stakes. I raised the stakes at the risk of humiliating myself completely.

The novel ending I performed at REDCAT was the previous one with the pregnancy scare. I read that to my peers. Changed the ending to something the more sordid herpes for my final thesis submission that I was afraid to admit even to myself. No wonder my professor Bruce Bauman seemed angry at me at my thesis review. Bauman knew I had slept with everyone.

It may have been a shitty thing to do but given my situation I did what I had to do and what I could. I try to be more ethical now. Now i just don't have sex without disclosing. I write about my herpes all the time so that everyone knows. It's just easier that way.

Future Fiction London put *Jet Set Desolate* on Amazon in 2009. Now anyone could find out my most closely guarded secret.

I forced myself to stop caring who knew I had herpes. I became flagrantly open about my STD status as a way to cope. Trying to scare away any potential fuck who had a problem with it before they ended up running out of my bed in the middle of the night. That happened once in early 2013. Never again.

I would far prefer that a potential sexual partner read about my herpes previously from a safe distance and come to terms with it before approaching me to save me the awkwardness of telling them.

Sometimes it's appreciated when someone speaks the unspeakable. That's what I'm into.

I amped my novel up with all I had. Left my herpes as an Easter egg that people would have to read my book to find. I'll use shameless tricks if I have to. If someone reads one of my books because they're trying to dig up dirt on me like I know some people do I invite them to.

I accept my herpes now because once again there's just no choice or cure, much like my mental illness.

As the Serenity Prayer says, "The wisdom to accept what I cannot change."

Sex was not fun when people got their feelings hurt. Dante, Daniel and I were all in classes together for two years. Inevitably, it got awkward.

I'm sure it will be inevitably far more awkward if and when Dante and Daniel read this. I'm so sorry, you guys. We always used condoms and I never had outbreaks at CalArts so I'm certain I did not give you my herpes. I'm so sorry you had to find out about it by reading about it.

I tell people now. Now I don't have casual sex anymore.

CalArts was in Valencia. An isolated desert suburban outpost that was mostly mall and Magic Mountain. Not a lot of youth culture or culture period besides what was available on campus. After living in the dorms in Valencia for a year, after awhile I just wanted to move to Los Angeles. North Hollywood was between the two. In the San Fernando Valley with all the porn and liquor stores. It seemed like a good compromise. So I moved to North Hollywood in September of 2007 when I returned from my parents house from a hot summer of leisure.

North Hollywood was its own city. Apart from Los Angeles. Separated by a range of mountains. Threaded by the 5, 101 and 170 freeways.

I didn't actually live in LA, proper, yet. I was isolated from Stephen and Alex in Koreatown. I comforted myself that the address "North Hollywood" sounded glamorous if one didn't live in or know anything about LA. Even if it really it wasn't actually Hollywood. North Hollywood lacked Hollywood's glitz. Glamour. Clubs. Stars on the sidewalk.

I went to Hollywood Boulevard sometimes. Browsed in that fabulous big costume store. Bought stripper lingerie I never wore. Walked past the Hollywood Wax Museum. Ripley's Believe It or Not with the neon marquees in big shapes. The Gay and Lesbian Center was on Schrader in Hollywood.

I got free therapy at The Gay and Lesbian Center for a bit in 2008 right after I graduated. My therapist was a young woman. An intern. She honestly seemed to like me. Wanted to help me in the beginning. Her untrained well-meaning nature was a bit of a disaster. This therapist thought that my drinking while taking Ativan was a form of slow suicide. Benzodiazepines and alcohol can kill you.

Taking all of my benzo's and drinking a lot was how my wife died. A suicide. A fast, shocking, unexpected one.

But Ativan and alcohol weren't killing me yet. I consumed both every day. I drank a lot. I was sad. I felt I had no future yet again.

I developed an even more severe anxiety disorder after the social fallout of my second year at CalArts. Worse then the anxiety episode I had with the break-in in San Diego in 2005. My over-burdened County Mental Health psychiatrist prescribed Ativan again in spring of 2008. I took Ativan every day until 2013.

I painfully detoxed off Ativan along with alcohol at Brotman Medical Center when I finally got sober.

In 2014 I was put back on Klonopin. It was safer once I had stopped drinking. I still take Klonopin twice a day. I hope to never again have to go off of it.

I named my first poetry book *Lorazepam & the Valley of Skin* after the Lorazepam that brought me so much joy. That and the flesh trade of North Hollywood that Nick was a part of. *Lorazepam & the Valley of Skin* was published in Sweden by my CalArts colleague Jacquelyn Davis in 2009.

I published two books in Europe the year after I got out of my MFA program. A novel and a book of poetry translated into Swedish.

I seemed to need benzodiazepines. I didn't do well when I was off them. My anxiety was just that bad. All of the psych meds worked a lot better once I stopped drinking in 2013.

I drank heavily and took prescribed Ativan from 2008 to 2013. It was fatal to take alcohol and Ativan together: I took them together for several years without dying. I courted death. My daily combo could have killed me at any time.

The therapist I had in 2008 at the Gay and Lesbian Center thought I should check into a hospital absolutely immediately because of the ongoing risk of taking Ativan and alcohol together. I was addicted to both.

My new therapist actually said she would send the police over to check on me the next morning if I did not go to the ER that night after our session. I drove to the ER desperately afraid of the police on her orders. I didn't know how I was going to pay for the hospital. I didn't have health insurance once I left CalArts.

My therapist called me as I was driving to the ER. Told me that she talked to her supervisor. I didn't have to go to the ER. This intern therapist felt I should move back in with my parents after grad school. She tried to accelerate me towards that. I didn't want to live with my parents again. This time there would be no more graduate school to rescue me away.

I had to stop seeing that therapist because it wasn't safe for me anymore. She was young. Rather alarmist. I felt she put me in danger when in actuality I was putting myself in danger. She was just the only one to notice it, as therapists usually are.

Even East Hollywood where I've lived since 2013 is kind of ghetto and dangerous. It was actually West Hollywood that the more desirable Hollywood to live in. West Hollywood was park-like. Nice but so expensive. Parking was difficult if not impossible. Maren and her husband River lived in West Hollywood in 2013 before moving into the Show Cave warehouse.

I didn't know any Hollywood info of that summer of 2007 when I moved to North Hollywood.

I did know that in North Hollywood, three Hollywood's over, I could actually afford a pretty big room with a walk in closet and it's own bathroom in a two-bedroom with a pool with my BFF. Vaulted ceilings. Balcony.

Rachel and I rented that unit the fall of 2007 even if it had carpet instead of the hardwood floors we wanted. Even if had slat blinds instead of the more elegant curtains I preferred. Even if the whole place was arranged around the pool so you could hear everyone that went down there in all of the apartments surrounding through the window.

I liked that apartment in the beginning. Total fishbowl. Total panopticon.

Rachel and I moved in. She unpacked her wedding presents. I moved in the antique Queen Anne bedroom set that my grandma Janet left me when she went into the old folks home. Bought a full mattress from IKEA, finally. I had furniture for the first time since San Francisco. It felt like a home.

I liked North Hollywood in the beginning. North Hollywood was home for two years. North Hollywood is in the San Fernando Valley. Next door sexy to Burbank. Sherman Oaks. Toluca Lake. Studio City.

It actually worked out to live in North Hollywood. Not a lot of famous people were from there so I was in the North Hollywood Wikipedia for a while. I inserted myself into the notable persons entry for North Hollywood. It took years for the Wikipedia Gods to realize I was an imposter and edit me out. I have a Wikigrain now partially because of that bold yet pathetic attempt.

I wanted to get into Wikipedia. Hells to the yes! That was a sign that one had arrived as a writer. I still hunger to get a Wikipedia in 2016. I am waiting for someone else to make me a Wikipedia entry. That's apparently how it works. My feeble attempts to give myself a Wikipedia entry on my boyfriend's account were shot down and deleted immediately because in 2009 I wasn't notable enough.

I am still nakedly ambitious. You have to be to keep doing all of this boring hard work for years and years with no paycheck.

I wanted to live in Los Angeles where all the culture was. The parties second-year music starlet Daiana Feuer threw. Yes, the parties. Shows. Bars. I lived in North Hollywood for two years trying to get close to Los Angeles before I finally moved to Silver Lake in 2010.

All the fun stripper stores lined the end of Hollywood Boulevard. I would look. Occasionally buy or just look, fascinated.

I wanted to affiliate myself with Hollywood. I liked the idea of it. The dream. It held a potent weight in the cultural subconscious. Especially if you had never been to LA. Knew Hollywood only through the movies and television as a magical place where dreams came true. I moved to North Hollywood to get as close to Hollywood as I could practically afford to get with a reasonable commute to school.

North Hollywood, as they say, has "All of the sleaze: None of the glamour."

Chapter 8 – SCHIZOPHRENIA

I went home for Christmas in December 2006. Regaled my parents with excited stories of things I was learning. Revolutionary new types of writing that they had never heard of. They humored my enthusiasm.

I brought along in the car a bulging tote bag of books. None of which I cracked as I was so busy talking. I talked through the long drive from Valencia to San Diego.

That Christmas dinner my mother, father and I got very drunk. I told them a lot of things that I did not expect to tell them including that I had done heroin before.

I was supposed to be housesitting for Rachel and Aaron's nice Hillcrest apartment that Aaron lived alone in during most of the year. Rachel and Aaron were in Barbados with Aaron's family for the holidays.

I retreated in embarrassment to their white one-bedroom. Lay on the white leather couch. Drank bottle after bottle of white wine. I didn't want to be around my parents. I wanted solitude.

My mother called me at Aaron's. I spoke with her. Assured her I wasn't doing drugs anymore. I just needed to be alone.

In January of 2007 I returned to CalArts. There I had a breakdown brought on by taking expired medication.

In the slender light of dawn in my dorm room. A cup of coffee by my hand. Just risen. Bathrobe on. The twitching began. Cramping. Twitching. My hand scrawled through the haiku. My arm thumped the table. My leg spasmed. I tripped on the table. Spilled my coffee.

What's going on? I wondered. I have to get dressed! I thought. They can't take me naked. They can't come in here. Find me all splayed out dead. Drooling. Naked.

I know I'm going away to the hospital. Fuck, I don't know for how long. I need to bring things. I need books if I'm going away.

I threw my *Art in Theory* anthology into my bag. Thought if I was in the psych ward I could at least read some Artaud. Followed it with *Last Exit to Brooklyn* and *The Bell Jar*. I grabbed a skirt and T-shirt and pulled them on. As a crowning touch to my Sunset Boulevard moment, I took hold of an ancient, deteriorating fur coat and draped it around myself.

Might as well go out kicking, I thought.

Barely able to control my body, I threw open my dorm room door into the dim dawn.

This is so embarrassing, I thought. Having a breakdown in my dorm room ? Going to my dorm-mate to drive me to the ER?

It's so meta that I'm so aware of how embarrassing this is. It's just so meta that I'm aware of being aware of how embarrassing this is. It's just all so meta…

Thoughts screamed through my brain. Cycling rapidly. The endless train of actions that were each more meta than the last. Endless cycling. Endless repetition.

Not the first psychiatric break I've had caused by critical theory. Much like my Baudrillard psychosis in *Scaffolding* in 1999. Probably won't be the last critical theory breakdown either.

I frantically groped my way down the hall. My body contorted violently. I threw myself at my dorm-mate Anne's door. I pounded. Screamed.

Anne drove me to the hospital.

On the floor of the emergency room waiting room, I thrashed around. My legs leapt widely to the side, exposing my leopard print underwear and tampon. The thought blurred up to me for a moment that I must look ridiculous. Disgusting.

“That’s so sad,” said a woman to another in the lobby. As my head pounded on the floor, I wondered if I was going to sustain brain damage.

“Couldn’t we put something underneath her, like her head?” asked Anne. She was strained.

“Finish the paperwork first, and then we’re take her in. I’ll need her date of birth? Address?”

I let out a garbled shriek. My body convulsed. Collapsed. My limbs slammed against the tile.

“I am fucking flipping out,” I screamed, “I need a sedative! All I need is a fucking sedative, and you people can’t give me one! What the hell sort of medical professionals are you? I am suffering! Watch me suffer. Someone fucking do something!”

“Please,” Anne turned to the paramedic.

I have Schizoaffective Disorder. That’s co-occurring Bipolar Disorder and Schizophrenia. Psych ward stays happen. Spiritual experiences happen. It is part of the illness. It is my cross to bear.

“Finish the paperwork,” said the paramedic in the ER in 2007. “We have to see if she’s faking just to get sedated. Some people drug-seek.”

I was unable to control my limbs. The convulsions hit in waves. Wellbutrin seizure. One wave died out to a few moments of tranquility. Another hit hard and violent. I tried to pull myself up on one arm on the chair. Anne offered me a glass of water. I fell back weakly. Limp. My arm thrashed. I spilled the cup of water in a gush across the tile. I lay in a pool of water. Writhed.

Finally, the paramedics came out with a stretcher. Loaded me in. They put a plastic sleeve on my finger. Stuck a needle into my vein.

At this point the events become blurry. I was sedated soon enough. After they questioned me, the convulsions gradually ceased. I felt warm, floating numbness lifting from the bottom of my body to my neck.

I talked to Anne as I felt fluctuating waves run through my body.

My mind was still circling with the endless reassessment of the meta. Everything could always be ever more meta.

Doctors kept coming in. They asked me questions. They marked things on clipboards.

I felt a surge of the sedative. I closed my eyes.

I floated over colored cubes. Patterns. Colors. Fields. The sky dark. I floated over fields of flowers. I was shuttered into darkness for a long time.

I saw a cartoon Jesus with his arms open and heaven behind him. Jesus was taking me. I must be dying.

I didn't believe in any Gods then. I didn't believe in heaven or hell. That couldn't be real. I must be imagining this. How ridiculous. I'd read one-too-many bad Reader's Digest near-death experiences and internalized the narrative.

No. Just no. It couldn't be true.

I saw a long tunnel with a white opening at the end. The tunnel was bifurcated and slashed with spirals and diamonds. Was I dying?

Suddenly I popped back through the tunnel. I opened my eyes.

Anne was still there, with her back to me, on the phone. She hung up. Curled up on the chair next to me. She reached out for my hand.

"What's going on in there?" she said.

"Better, I think." I stared up at the hospital curtain. An IV hung from my arm. There was a Band-Aid over cotton on my inner arm from another wound.

I looked at the curtain again. Hallucinated the Grim Reaper. Skeletal. Grimacing in a black cloak. Staring at me. Beckoning with one finger. A green and red tentacle from some unseen monstrous beast arched above. Hell had come to claim me. I must be dying. Still.

"Wait a sec? Is that skeleton really there?"

"Nothing's there, sweetie. It's just the curtain"

"Oh, wait… Can you move the curtain? Please! Please make it go away."

I gripped Anne's hand.

I said, "I'm dying. I'm dying. This is my deathbed. Please. I'm so glad you're here with me. I'm glad that someone is here with me. Thank you." Anne contorted her forehead in pain.

I saw upon the white wall of the small room a train of little angels that looked like cartoon Strawberry Shortcake children. They lowered themselves down from Heaven. Body by tiny body they climbed. Formed a Jacob's ladder of bodies. My angels reached out arms and hands. Looked for me. Came back for me. Found me. I stretched my arms above me as far as I could. I cried out for Jesus to come save me. I thrashed. I kicked. I begged.

"We will restrain you if you don't calm down," the hospital orderly said above me.

"But… God?"

"Would you like to speak to the hospital chaplain later?"

"Yes!"

I fell back again. Turned to see that the Grim Reaper was still there. Nothing I could do could make him go away. He was there when I squeezed my eyes shut. Only to see the battle between Heaven and Hell over my soul. The Grim Reaper was there again when I opened my eyes to see the battle over my soul played out all around me on the wall of my hospital room in a hallucination like a projection that only I could see. I was the only one who could see any of this. I really believed that I was dying.

There would be moments when Jehovah decided to accept me. He welcomed me. Then suddenly, he had a change of heart. Ran into something in my back file. Bisexuality. That abortion when I wanted to finish college. Promiscuity. Drug addiction. I had a few sins on my plate.

Jehovah kicked me back down to hell again.

Was I better off with Satan? Hell looked like the best party ever. Flames. Red and orange like a bar. All the most interesting people were there. I rode through hell in a little cart like a Disneyland ride. I was going through hell in a veritable hand-basket

There are many Gods to worship. I follow a neo-pagan pantheon now. Did I want to worship this God, Jehovah? A God who would hang me out to dry only to be rescued later at his whim?

I cried out. The Gods were at war over me in the ER. I begged. Groveled. Attendants came in. Shoved more and more anti-psychotics into my veins through the IV.

Finally, a clipboard was shoved onto my lap with a form I couldn't read and a black BIC pen.

"What does this say?" I said.

"They're going to help you," said the nurse. "This will let them help you."

"Anything, anything to make this stop."

I sighed. I signed it. Felt a surge of warm numbness. Passed out.

I awoke some time later in a narrow, hard bed. The room had no furniture. I padded down the hard linoleum floor in my bare feet. My shoes and belt were gone.

I saw a man with a frothy white mustache. I walked up to him shyly.

"Hey. Um. Could you tell me where I am?"

"You're in the Henry Mayo Psych Ward."

"Oh shit. What was I brought in for? What was all that?"

"Oh, you were the one that was all thrashing around. Yes, I've been looking at your chart. You have hysteria."

"Hysteria? You mean like Freud, Charcot?" I did my reading on hysteria on the Internet in San Diego in 2006. I knew all how the hysteria diagnosis was used to exploit and imprison so many women for the entertainment of male doctors in the 1800s. Old psychiatry. Bad psychiatry.

My writing drew from the myth of hysteria indirectly. I did not expect it to so directly intersect my life.

"You know, or maybe you wouldn't know," the male doctor said. "It's when women get these things that happen to them for which there's no rational explanation. You have hysteria, my dear."

The doctor walked away.

I stayed in the Henry Mayo Psych Ward in Valencia for five days. Rachel visited me twice a day. The writing program sent flowers. I wasn't allowed to have the thorny blooms. I had been in the psych ward before. I pretty much knew what to do to get out in a timely fashion. Just start dressing normally and wearing makeup. Don't act out, yell, resist or throw things. Eventually after the seventy-two hour hold is up they will let you go. And they did.

I remember Rachel picking me up. The immense freedom that Valencia seemed to hold as we drove away from the hospital.

I came back to CalArts. Began to talk and write about what had happened. People began to draw away from me.

I was already becoming a bit of a problem with the program.

There was an incident when I took a Klonopin from Omar right before a reading. Drank too much after the reading as I tended to do at CalArts. Hit on the Program Assistant. Pissed my dress on the Butler Building couch. Was apprehended by the ambulance drivers after being walked to my dorm room. Ended up in the hospital for an alcohol overdose.

I told the doctor's at the ER that I was a thirty year old grad student with no car living on campus and really had no place to blow off any of the immense stress that I felt. So that's why I was drinking excessively on campus.

The Valencia ER released me to Omar. He took me back to his place. Put me to bed.

I entwined my legs with his in his bed. My piss-stained thighs.

Omar said "No, Andrea."

I never tried to sleep with Omar again. I had to learn to stop trying to sleep with my friends. Some lessons came with time.

I was put on Ativan again and Lexapro, this time in 2007. The Wellbutrin I was on supposedly caused the seizure. I was going to San Fernando Valley Mental Health, another public clinic. I had a good psychiatrist. I was trying to make it through my MFA with a serious health condition. It was hard.

My Schizoaffective Disorder kicked in in full force. I heard a lot of voices talking about me when I was on campus. I didn't even consider that I might be hearing voices that were in my head. I assumed that everything I heard was gossip and everyone was talking about me.

I now regret the attacks I subjected my classmates to. I thought I had overheard them talking about me. Now I don't know what I had really heard.

I had a lot of anger. I heard a lot of anger.

I should have gone to rehab between San Francisco and Valencia so that I could readily attack the MFA. I didn't so I still had heavy substance abuse problems.

I met this filmmaker at the first year CalArts Halloween party in 2006. The crazy night ended with me having a hot tub threesome with him and his friend in a big house in Saugus where he rented a room from a family. Tons of coke. I found a coke and fuck-buddy.

Not so good for me but so fun for me. That bond would hold us for a while although he was not boyfriend material, nor was he interested in that.

By the end of the second year of my MFA in 2008 I was doing coke with my South American filmmaker in his sub-level studio. Languid evenings of conversation about his film. Hasty sex on the studio couch. He had an enormous dick. Used Magnums. I had amazing sex with him off and on for several years afterwards until we drifted apart. He refused my Facebook friend request later. Probably for the best. Such friends are dangerous.

That whole time I was at CalArts from 2006-2008, in the collective experience with all of those young artists, I thought I was hearing my classmates, friends and fuck-buddy's thoughts. Favorable or unfavorable. I heard a lot of shit. Heard voices in a hallucinatory stew like the experimental writing word salads I wrote. Hearing voices was a sign of Schizoaffective Disorder manifesting before it was officially diagnosed in 2011. These thoughts were considered paranoid by my psychiatrists.

I could still hear what I thought were people's thoughts on occasion. When I first became a witch I was sure my Schizoaffective Disorder made me psychic and allowed me to talk to ghosts. A blessing and a curse.

I learned from an article in Slate that the voice that I hear are actually subvocal speech. A different part of my brain talking to me deep in my throat about what I thought people were thinking about me. Projecting my worse fears and most grandiose fantasies onto the white walls of my Hollywood apartment.

I heard voices much less now that I took my Saphris regularly and didn't drink.

Unless of course the wild edge of sleep deprivation to finish a book edit ran me past the limit of the point if the night or morning. Passing pre-bed psychosis sometimes happened if I drank too much coffee and stayed up too late. I tried not to do it but so often the work seemed to demand it. I thrived off of sleep deprivation. Sometimes the voices in my head told me good, kind, affirming things. I told myself that I was hallucinating what I wanted to hear.

It was all in my head, as mental illness is.

I was aware that I played with fire.

June 2016 I stayed up a whole 26 hours working on what I hoped would be a final edit of this novel. I knew it would not be my last pass. I worked fervently, doggedly into the night. Ignored the voices and rainbow pixels until I could no longer at two am.

I took my Saphris. Tucked myself into bed. I still could't sleep for a long time. I kept writing and editing on my laptop in bed.

It's possible that I have psychic abilities now brought on by my PTSD and Schizophrenia. I'm not ruling it out. I know all of the magic I take such solace in may just be another Schizoaffective Delusion.

I still sometimes think I can hear people's thoughts when they are thinking about me.

I read the tarot often. My friendly voices along with the tarot definition pamphlet tell me what the cards mean

That trip to the psych ward after a spiritual hallucination and seizure confirmed that I was crazy to my class in January 2007. I was thought to be dangerous in my MFA Program. My peers began to avoid me. I had "persecution mania." I thought everyone at CalArts was out to get me. Plotting against me.

In actuality my CalArts peers probably felt sorry for me. Were worried. Concerned. Yet there wasn't much that they could do. Not much anyone even my friends could do. I was still such a raw alcoholic hot mess.

My antipsychotics weren't working because I was drinking so much in order to not care about what I was hearing and still believe in myself enough to go on with the program. I thought my classmates and friends were talking shit about me all the time the second year as the Schizoaffective symptoms intensified. It really messed up my relationships with them. I had some friends in the program until the symptoms set in.

I confronted other writers like Sara Finnerty for talking shit about me down the long echoing corridors. Sparking a rift when this gentle YA writer was kind to me before. I could not tell if the whispers I was hearing were overheard or hallucinations. I believed everything I heard in the beginning of my illness. I didn't know I was hearing voices.

Who knows what is real? I certainly don't.

I may have been hearing people's thoughts. I thought I heard what people really thought about me said in my head whether or not it had actually come out of their mouths at that last year at CalArts.

Chapter 9 — SECOND YEAR ALIENATION

Who was I to know that between twenty writers most of them wouldn't really want to talk to me or see me at all by CalArts graduation in 2008. My alcoholism. Adderall abuse. Promiscuity. Mental Illness. My competitive, egomaniacal nature.

I was not too pleasant to be around as the two years wore on. I slept with almost all the guys. Emotionally and financially exhausted the women.

I just poured out all over the place wherever you put me. Hot mess. Portrait of the artist as a desperate cougar.

I put myself out there is your face at CalArts. That's where I learned how to do what I do. My classmates got really tired of my high jinx. Ten years later they kept me at the distance of the Internet and submitted writing. That was a comfortable boundary after what we all had been through together.

I know I'm a high-maintenance pain in the ass.

I try not to be too much of a diva because it's not professional. I know that now. Some of these lessons take time. My MFA was a decade ago. I'm only just now coming to terms with and writing about the experience.

I read a lot in the Sprawl Reading series between 2006-2008. Published in the *Sprawl Journal* that Janice Lee hand-bound for AWP in New York. Published in *Artizen*, the student magazine that Daiana Feuer edited. Well-connected hipster Daiana got Urb to review *Artizen*. Exciting for us back at CalArts.

I wanted blindly and rapaciously to be famous. I would sleep my way there at the slightest provocation.

I offered to sleep with my Independent Study professor Stephen Barber who eventually got *Jet Set Desolate* published. I thought it was called for given what he had offered to do for me. I was used to things being transactional. Barber politely turned me down. Sex wasn't necessary.

The "most dangerous man in Britain" as Stephen Barber was called by the Independent just loved my novel. He began letting his wife linger in the office during our sessions. We studied Antonin Artaud fervently. Bless him for protecting me from my own desperate ambition.

Stephen Barber got *Jet Set Desolate* published anyway in 2009.

My writing was pornographic. Violent. Punishing. Assaultive. After a certain point, some my colleagues didn't want to see any more of it. What Barber and Viegener loved was scaring others. More delicate souls like sweet Jennifer Hawe asked the professors to not have to read my work because it was too triggering for them. I understand that now although at the time I was offended.

I was producing so much writing. It just kept coming. Much of *Angelina at the Serrano* was written at CalArts although I put it all together ten years later. The two manuscripts I came into the program with were a novella and a novel. Both were unpublished. Seemed unpublishable.

I briefly worked my books a little ways through in an amateur critique group in San Francisco where I was judged and judged hard for my lifestyle. A friendly if busy professional woman's critique group in San Diego.

My two novels were still not really all that sifted through. My manuscripts were sloppy. Poorly proofread because I had to be drunk to even face the material. Pornographic. Confessional. Displaying a shocking lack of boundaries. Much of my manuscripts were written while drunk or on coke.

When I combined the novella and novel directed by Matias the manuscript came to 450 pages. I confronted everyone in my class with a printout of my manuscript in its entirety for each one of them to read at their leisure early on it the first year. The confrontation of all of those manuscript pages sitting there on the classroom table as my colleagues walked in. No wonder they didn't like me.

My novel professor requested that I give the manuscript to everyone all at once as there was so much of it. Steve Erickson, whom I read and worshipped in the nineties. I did what he said. It was a lot of text to get through. More repetitive drugs and sex than anyone could really handle then look me in the eye in class the next day.

The second year of my MFA Program things changed. Fatigue and social coldness set in with my peers in the Critical Studies Department. I lost Rachel's friendship by the second year. No one in the writing program would even really give me the time of day.

No-one except for Anne Marie Kinney. I TA'D with her. Even Anne-Marie got pretty frustrated with my mental illness. Talkativeness. Flakiness.

Anne-Marie and I carpooled that second year. 2007-2008. It was about thirty miles to CalArts from Los Angeles. We both lived in North Hollywood. It took forty-five minutes on the 5 Freeway to get from Los Angeles to Valencia. We talked a lot on that drive. I unloaded a lot of my anguish on Anne-Marie.

A fatigue set in with my peers and me. By that time everyone in the writing program was already reading several books a week in different classes. They were reading, commenting on and putting to workshop text in other genres. Writing papers. Painting. Acting. Playing music. Whatever their other metier's were.

My incessant writing produced more labor for them. Everyone gets tired. Worked that hard for two years. I got tired.

I was exhausted by the time our class went to AWP in New York January 2008. A fundraising effort heroically spearheaded by Janice. I got so sick when I came back the New York snow that I took a week off school.

I called Matias at home in the middle of my crisis.

Said I was "hanging by a thread."

Matias had me come in to talk to Brigde Mullens, the sympathetic then-head of the writing program. I changed all my classes to Independent Studies. Only drove to CalArts once a week to teach after that. It was finally all too much.

My peers and I separated my second year. I I was dating an abusive drunken transgender prostitute named Nick who lived with me in the North Hollywood apartment I had shared with Rachel. She moved out partially through my second year.

2008. I was a skeleton by then. I was sick and sad.

My friends were Stephen van Dyck. Omar Routher. Alex Castle. Gay male friends only once I lost the support of my peers in the writing program. I couldn't sleep with them and fuck it up.

"Don't fuck it up," says RuPaul. I definitely did fuck it up at CalArts.

My last semester at CalArts in 2008 was very dark. My writing was everywhere. So nakedly personal. In *Artizen.* Being read at Sprawl. I wrote explicit sex scenes. Explicit rape scenes. People began to ask for permission not to read my work. Those who had already seen me naked recoiled, repulsed.

I had a lot of painful experiences that I was processing. I was working through my experiences in Portland and San Francisco. Some of those were very dark. Darkly glamorous? Drug addiction. Alcoholism. Sex. Sex work. I was perpetually putting in workshop the manuscripts that were to become my *Jet Set Desolate* and *Angelina at the Serrano*.

In my writing I was working out painful things. My pain struck chords within people, whether in sympathy or revulsion at something within themselves that they no longer wanted to touch. I just kept producing more and more of it. In the small MFA program we were all getting really sick of each other.

I was still compulsively promiscuous as I have always been but this time I was thirty. A baby cougar. In charge so I felt in my mounting delusions. Feeling desirable but getting older. I needed to get laid at CalArts. I was unwillingly celibate for two years while in San Diego. I had a lot of things I needed to get out of my system and work out at the expense of everyone around me.

I was just so immersed in my writing. Learning how to read and perform.

I went back to sleeping my way through my class after Thursday night Sprawl readings. That lovely foreign student Ashraf from Morocco. That was unexpected. I discovered if I hung out after the reading for long enough I could find someone to sleep with.

I saw great experimental theatre at CalArts. Animation. Readings. Films. Dance performances. All on campus for the most part.

While at CalArts, I showed the *Jet Set Desolate* manuscript to Steve Erickson. He liked it. Erickson liked my work, I remember. He sent me an long encouraging email when he finished my book.

Steve Erickson emailed to me "I guess what I want to say to you is that in many ways, Andrea, is that of all the first-year students, you look the most to me like a real writer: you have the talent and you have the drive." I saved that email in my old yahoo inbox to this day. Reread it when I needed encouragement. His words meant so much to me.

Steve Erickson's *Arc D'X* was the whole reason I wanted to go to CalArts in the first place. Erickson taught novel at CalArts. He was like a lighthouse to me. As soon as I got there the first day of registration for his second-year's only novel class I showed up ridiculously early and embarrassingly often to pester the administrator until I got into the class.

That day in novel class when Steve Erickson said "This is first rate!" of chapters that became part of *Angelina at the Serrano.* I left the classroom in a haze of bliss. Called my mom to gush.

My other novel professor, Bruce Bauman, didn't seem to like my work much. I do a niche sort of thing.

Anne-Marie said to me in the car, "You have to know that only some people are going to be into your writing." She was right.

Bruce said in workshop, "You can hear all of these stories if you just go to an AA meeting." He was right, although I didn't know it at the time. Bauman tried so hard with me. I know I was a difficult student. I have wanted to apologize to him for ten years. Maybe he'll read this.

I finally did apologize to Bruce Bauman on a Facebook comment in 2016. Bauman said in a response comment that it was fine. He was happy I was well and writing.

This book is intended to function as an explanation and apology for so many things I regret.

Queer Kathy Acker scholar Matias Viegener did like my work. He was my mentor along with Stephen Barber. I didn't try to sleep with him because he was gay. I had learned that lesson by now.

I TA-ed for Viegener for Contemporary Literature. My first and only experience teaching that wasn't a total shit-show.

Stephen Barber was the visiting Antonin Artaud scholar from the UK whom I did an Independent Study with. Barber liked my book so much that he handed it off to the right editor to get it published in the UK in 2009.

Jet Set Desolate was published by Future Fiction London. A short-lived imprint of Barber's publisher Creation Books helmed by my idol Hillary Raphael. Both presses are long out of business in 2016. Raphael had three children and couldn't put in the time or money anymore. Creation Books had been doing it for ten years and finally threw in the towel as people must.

I have always been thankful that Hillary Raphael set my book up on Amazon print-on-demand so it didn't seem to be going out of print as I expected that it would. I will never see any royalties but I accept that. Royalties might complicate my SSDI anyway.

I was one of the first of my class to publish, to a deafening silence. Publishing *Jet Set Desolate* didn't bring me the satisfaction or fame that I expected for seven years while I wrote it. in San Francisco and San Diego. The press that came to Anne-Marie.

Publishing my first two books in Europe right out of my MFA program were still some of the best things that ever happened to me. Up there with getting lavishly gay married via winning a contest to the love of my life in 2011.

Best things that ever happened to me up there with getting my impossible $100,000 student loans forgiven for being "Totally and Permanently Disabled" in 2014. I have to pay it all back if I ever go off of SSDI. There is a $100,000 penalty to me making money or getting a job that makes more than $1,000 a month in 2016. With that constraint I write for free for the Internet and small presses. Sell my paintings cheaply if ever to friends. Stay low. Try to go for slow burn DIY. Get the work out there with whomever will take it.

I can't afford to make money from writing or art, although they are my life. I am lucky to have a wealthy family because without them I would be homeless.

My situation is paradoxical. Cruel. Lovely. I must accept the caveats that comes with the blessings.

The few times I tried to get an agent they didn't seem interested but I never tried very hard. I couldn't afford to get an advance. Owing my student loans again would put me in more debt than I started out with. The renewed debt wouldn't be worth the glory.

I waited on slow burn for seven years for *Jet Set Desolate* to become what I so hoped was a cult classic. It got converted into several free ebooks that I never saw any royalties from. J*et Set Desolate* was in the past. Out of my hands.

I spent a lot of time pouring my squalid vulnerabilities out to Twitter before people began to notice me in 2014. I social media networked relentlessly with small presses, journals and editors in 2016. Hoped that I wasn't annoying. I probably am.

At CalArts Graduation no one would speak to me except the filmmaker I was sleeping with and Mark So. We split a couple bottles of champagne. No glasses. I stood extra tall in my platform heels and near-transparent sack-dress. Decided I would be the one publishing my thesis within the year.

I did.

I was drunk on my own ego because it was the only bottle open to me. No one else was passing their flask my way except Dante. My entire class would not speak to me.

When I came to CalArts I was so starry-eyed and full of hopes and ambition and dreams.

I got a $70,000 fuck you and an amazing education because I liked to write about cocaine, drunk bitches and disco trash. No, and it wasn't conceptual or experimental enough either. Or tame enough to be young adult. I was also a bit, no, just a bit mouthy in workshop.

Admittedly. Admittedly. Admittedly. I let that Bipolar rage out of the cage on more than a few occasions.

That was likely what had brought me to the point of slugging down Veuve Clicquot with these two people I barely knew at graduation in 2008. Knowing one would likely pull this dress off later in his sub-level studio once we'd worked our way through a gram.

On my desk in 2016 is a magnet of a pulp novel cover. Its lurid illustration: a couple moving in with an, "AC/DC" (read, bisexual) lesbian, and "surrendering to an orgy of lust!" It was a housewarming gift from Rachel in 2007.

I though the magnet t was funny and cute at the time before everything went south. Sour. Sad. Tears were shed. Rachel and I said goodbye forever later in 2007.

That magnet is still on my desk holding up some postcards but I can't quite get myself to touch it. I can't quite get myself to look at it, squarely, or do much with it at all.

What reads sadder about the magnet is that the devotion I gave Rachel was a love more queer than BFF. A love better given to a girlfriend. Wasted on her. When she left that North Hollywood apartment my heart was broken. But I always love my friends like this. In the end it's best that we don't become lovers.

I still wonder sometimes if a triad with Rachel and her husband was what they really wanted from me. Had I been simply been so dimwitted as to be unable to comply with their plans when it really came down to it? Or did they just want a drinking and dinner companion? Rachel and Aaron were lovely, delightful people. We had a lovely friendship. But eventually I started dating Nick because I wanted my own man.

Rachel and Aaron were lost to me. They were as Atlantis. A lost continent. The two were getting a divorce when Rachel moved out to

Burbank with her filmmaker after CalArts. I saw on Facebook that Aaron was scattered across the country with a professorship in North Carolina never to be seen again.

Every relationship has a lifetime. It's healthy to realize that. It took time to realize that.

Anne-Marie and I traded off driving to Valencia from North Hollywood my second year at CalArts.

I went to Anne-Marie's wedding the summer between the two years of CalArts. She went to mine in 2011.

In 2009 when *Jet Set Desolate* came out, Anne-Marie sold a book via literary agent called *Radio Iris.* For a while she got what seemed like famous. Anne-Marie got a lot of publicity. I got very jealous. The writer's curse.

I distanced myself from Anne-Marie when she got famous and I didn't. We drifted anyway once CalArts was over as I drifted from everyone. I regret my distancing now. I was just so jealous. My first two books were only published on small presses in Europe. My books didn't get even a fraction of the press hers did. I realize now how petty that was. Jealousy can ruin friendships.

Anne-Marie had a daughter with her amiable husband after her first book came out. I looked at her website June 2016 when I was researching other author websites to better finesse my own. Saw that despite the agent and all the great press from *Radio Iris*, the last date on the website was 2013.

My jealousy weakened into compassion. I learned the cruel lesson of what happens when a writer has children. No one can do it all and still do it well.

I resolved never to have children as I had so many times before.

Anne-Marie in her domestic bliss was probably happier then me anyway in that she no longer felt the need to play this futile game.

Anne-Marie always was way more stable than I was.

I hoped Anne-Marie would write another icicle-cold brilliant book once her daughter was old enough. I would wait for it.

I didn't want to do the work that having a child had to be

I have a different attitude towards my classmate's publications now. The jealousy dissolved into support. I bought Joe Milazzo's *Crepuscule with Nellie* as soon as it came out. It sits on my coffee table beckoning for the moment when I will read it. I bought and read Maxi Kim's, Dante's Zuniga-West and Janice Lee's books.

A rising tide lifts all boats.

I understand now as I did not a decade ago that my colleagues at CalArts are part of the CalArts mafia that runs literary Los Angeles. It is best that I put old resentments behind me. They are useless now. We are each other's community, or part of it.

I still avoid readings because I am socially awkward in person. Reclusive. I'm much more articulate on the page or on the Internet. I'm so scared of bursting my delusional bubble that I'm quasi-famous that I don't go out. I'm so scared of running into someone who has read my Twitter or writings. I'm so scared of being laughed at or talked about. I'm sometimes so humiliated by how much I put out there that I rarely go to events. It's really something I need to get over.

Chapter 10 – FLASH FORWARDS TO DETOX

Four years passed. I married a woman named Katie Jacobson. She committed suicide after a year of marriage. All of that is the subject of a book called *Katie Rising* which covers 2009-2012.

I am skipping ahead to 2013-2016. My recovery from the addiction and alcoholism which plagued the first half of this book.

In January of 2013 I moved into a one-bedroom in Hollywood. My wife died October 15, 2012.

I just couldn't stay in that death trap of the one bedroom in Echo Park that we once had a life in. Drinking myself to death among the wilted funeral flowers. I needed to move. I needed to try to start again from zero.

This was before I got sober. Before I met Bobby.

These were desperate times. I hunted for apartments. I used padmapper.com. I quickly realized I couldn't afford to live in Echo Park or Silver Lake any more for the amount my parents allotted me for moving expenses. That had seemed like enough money to me, but rents went up. I would no longer be splitting the one-bedroom with a partner. I would be living alone for the first time in many years.

I wondered if I would be happy.

I had my cat, Nevada Jacobson-Cosentino. Her last name was hyphenated with my wife's as we got her together. The cat would live with me in Hollywood.

Hollywood, it would have to be. Hollywood was more dangerous, but it at least sounded glamorous. It sounded good if you had never actually been to LA.

Hollywood, Tinsel-town. The lost legends. I was willing to give living there a try.

I just didn't want to live in Koreatown. Definitely. I could actually afford a one-bedroom in Hollywood. Katie and I lived in a one-bedroom together in Echo Park. With all the stuff I inherited from my marriage as a one-bedroom was preferable.

I was thankful my parents allowed this.

My parents paid for my apartment, car insurance, gas, car repairs and psychiatric care. At this point they were so rich and old that they preferred to travel the world together and live together as a couple in that San Diego house near the beach without me. I was boundlessly, endlessly thankful that they preferred things to be this way as did I. I deeply enjoyed living alone and having an autonomous life, friends and relationships as I did not in 2005.

The sad year of recovery in my parents house in 2005 from the mistakes of the previous five years in San Diego was necessary. I so hoped in 2016 not to repeat living with my parents again. They seemed to prefer not living with me enough that they were willing to pay for me to live in Los Angeles.

To preserve my newfound happiness I stayed sober. Solvent. Stable. Responsible. As I faced down my forties I hoped to reserve the stability I had only so recently squared by staying out of dangerous entanglements even if that meant being alone most of the time.

I really enjoyed being alone in that apartment in Hollywood. Alone in my apartment became my paradise. Alone in my apartment became the new normal. I was happy that way.

In Los Angeles in 2007 I drove away from a little shoebox theatre on Hollywood with my mother in the car. We saw David Sedaris' one-man show about the Santa's Elf at Macy's. The neon was haunting. The voices of a choir on the corner by the Chinese Theatre. My eye filled with tears with the beauty of their song.

Koreatown was dangerous. When I moved to Hollywood in 2013 I was right next to Koreatown.

I moved to Hel-Mel. Hel-Mel within rental prices was still considered Koreatown. Hel-Mel was next to Silver Lake and West Hollywood, areas I preferred.

My ex-boyfriend Nick used to live in Koreatown with Stephen and Alex. This filthy boys apartment on Alexandria St. where my Katie and my band Cherry Ames Army Nurse played a show in 2009. Nick went out into the night drunk and on speed and he got mugged. His black boots from Melrose were stolen.

Whenever I would visit the boys in their smoky, dirty dishes crack-den in Koreatown, it would always be fun. However dirty, I kept coming over. They threw crazy amazing parties. There was never any parking.

I got so many parking tickets when I was dating Nick that I had him move in with me in 2007 mainly so I could stop getting parking tickets. What a mistake that was. Moving Nick in essentially cost me my relationship with Rachel.

Koreatown. It was so impacted. Like San Francisco. So corroded and dirty. Even in Hollywood. Some apartments I looked at were in terrifying areas there. So sketchy.

There are definitely nicer and less nice parts of Hollywood. Mostly West Hollywood is really nice. North Hollywood can be. I was priced out of West and into East Hollywood, however. Still kind of ghetto.

I didn't even do the interview for one apartment in East Hollywood. I just I just walked into the lobby. Saw all the surveillance cameras.

I walked out so there saying "Oh hell no."

My parents were quite generous with me now that my wife was dead. They paid the $400 for the movers. Allocated me a $1300 stipend monthly. I was thankful.

I dressed in a black and gold sweater. Black patterned slacks. My huge diamond wedding ring. Convinced the amiable designer landlord that both my parents could cosign. I presented myself as a disabled, widowed writer with a CalArts MFA. That was true.

I rented my dream apartment. A spacious one-bedroom in Hollywood with high ceilings. Hardwood floors. Crown molding. Retro fixtures. Air conditioning. Cockroaches as I later discovered.

I moved to an address not recognized as by the US Post Office or Google maps. I decided I lived in a magical vortex. My apartment in the Hel-Mel district of Hollywood was extremely private. There was no door buzzer. Two gates between me and the outside world. It was designed for private luxury. Big hardwood floored one-bedroom with white walls. Red and green tiles in the neatly stenciled green bathroom.

I decided I would happily live there until I died. I loved that apartment. Home.

It was when my wife Katie died in 2012 that my drinking really spiraled out of control. I was a problem drinker for many years. A drug addict for many years as well.

After I lost contact with that CalArts filmmaker I stopped having cocaine accessible to me and stopped doing it. Meth was undesirable and out of the picture by 2012. I was trying to be healthier.

I found Katie's corpse in bed with me when I woke up October 15, 2012. A prescription pill suicide. It filled me with a desire to blot out all memories with gin. Vodka. Whiskey. Wine. Preferably all in a series.

I would start at three in the afternoon. Sometimes as early as eleven every day. I existed on a schedule of indulgence. What I wanted I would have. I suffered profound loss. I lost what I loved the most. There was nothing left. I had nothing left in my life. Katie was gone.

I moved into a one-bedroom in East Hollywood. Holed myself up to drink myself to death.

But then something stopped me. It was a rising sense of misery, of shame. I was thirty-six in 2013. I felt my life had wasted away to nothing.

Even though I feared I essentially drove Katie to her death with my alcoholism and madness, she chose to take her own life. Her East Coast friend showed me her LiveJournal entry about always wanting to die by suicide. Suicide was always her plan. I wondered if this denouement was what she really wanted. I wondered so many things about Katie now that she was gone.

Katie and I for a dazzling four years had something beautiful. She chose to take that away. She was gone now. I was alone. I was more alone now than I had ever been in my life.

My friends were worried about me, but they drew back. Stephen sent me an email saying he couldn't hang out with me until I stopped drinking. Gabriel the same. Damian completely disappeared. Omar was very busy with his new boyfriend.

I hung out with Maren and her husband River quite a lot. They came over almost every night in the beginning until I didn't need them to anymore. We drank and smoked weed late into the night. Every once in a while Omar or Alex and I got together and smoked pot, but that was rare. The busy social whir I had with Katie dried up.

I had to donate the bunny rabbit Katie and I owned together to the pound before I moved into my new Hollywood apartment. My mother insisted. The bunny chewed up all of the wiring in the Echo Park place, creating a fire hazard. His cage was smelly and messy.

I got a tattoo of the rabbit on my thigh to remember it and Katie by.

All I did for six months was sit in that apartment and drink. I went through a shocking amount of alcohol. I bloated up. Lost the ability to cook. Read. Edit. Write. I couldn't go anywhere past four o'clock. My medication wasn't working very well. The voices in my head were loud.

On March 18, 2013, I drove to see my psychiatrist at Northeast Mental Health. I began to have delirium tremens driving down my cross street. Speeding up. Slowing down. Spasming. Jerking around in the car. I realized quickly I was unable to drive.

I pulled over into a one-hour zone. Got out of the car. Walked the long block home. It was the longest walk I'd ever taken.

I shook. Twitched. I had the shakes.

Alcohol withdrawal. It was three in the afternoon. I needed a drink but I had to see my psychiatrist to get more medication for the month. I was afraid I was going to have a seizure.

I got to my apartment. Lay on the couch frantically dialing 911 and staring at the number. I couldn't believe I was actually going to have to call an ambulance. I wouldn't stop shaking. I was terrified. I kept shaking. I called 911.

The ambulance came. I could see the scorn in the EMT's eyes as the turned me over to the ER.

"She's here for alcohol withdrawals," the EMT said at the hospital. Late afternoon sunshine on my shameful face. I felt so sick and wrong.

In those early years in San Francisco we never called ambulances. Now I really needed help.

The next day I checked myself into Brotman Medical Center for a medically sponsored detox. Brotman was the first detox I found in Los Angeles that took Medicare, my SSDI-provided health insurance. I could actually afford to detox now. I knew I had to get help.

Detox was a humbling experience. I was in there with all kinds of different addicts. At first it was very intimidating. There were a lot of loud people in the day room. Troubled people going through difficult things.

I stumbled into the day room in my hospital scrubs. A man with a sleek black pompadour came towards me with a welcoming hand.

"Hi! I'm Richard. Would you like some cranberry juice?"

"Sure! Thanks. I'm Lena."

"Have a seat."

We began to talk. I learned he had a fiancé on the outside that he was detoxing for. We learned a lot about each other over the next few days. At one point he even suggested sneaking into my room at night. I vetoed that. I was so heavily medicated that I barely knew what was going on, but I knew I was there to get sober, not to hook up. I wasn't over Katie. I wasn't ready.

Richard took me under his wing. When he left I had made other detox friends and felt more comfortable.

I shared a room with a homeless meth addict. She was kind to me. I overheard her intake. She was smoking crystal meth like I used to in San Francisco in 2004. We called it speed back then.

I discovered that a lot of these people were interesting to talk to. Naively I talked to them.

When I checked in the nurse said, "Now, there are a lot of interesting people in here. Keep your boundaries up." I tried to but it was hard. I had been so lonely since Katie's death. I comforted me to talk to these people not realizing how dangerous they were.

We had AA groups. Panels. Group therapy.

There were three square meals a day on little trays. Mediocre hospital food but not awful. Edible. Nourishing. I ate all of my meals.

There were four cigarette breaks in our days. I stood outside just for the sake of standing outside. To see the sky. I didn't smoke. I made conversation with the others.

Greg was another man I met in detox. We began chatting on smoke breaks. Greg was a hulking broad shouldered heroin addict with prison tattoos on his arms, hands and neck. He had done five years for armed robbery and assault. Giant pentagram on his left hand. Skull on his right. Letters on his knuckles spelling badass. Greg smoked Marlboro Lights. Talked to me in a low mutter. Complimented me on my makeup and clothes.

I had had the presence of mind to pack for detox. Took much comfort in doing my face. Blush and highlighter were my only defense against the ashen pallor of my alcoholic skin. My healthy glow was faked. The nurses believed it. I was so glad I brought clothes and make-up. Most people there showed up on the tail end of benders. Had only the clothes on their back. No makeup.

Lish told me later she was initially attracted to me as a future friend in Brotman because I was so well-dressed and made up unlike everyone else there. I was an easy mark for sure.

We circled in the smoke break alcove in Culver City by the side of the hospital around the tree and the chain link fence. We were a small group: Greg, the other addicts and alcoholics and I.

We sidled close. Greg and I talked about going to Venice Beach when we got out. We never did. I lost track of Greg after detox. Probably for the best.

The nurse whistled. We all followed her up the elevator to the ward. Dispersed down the hallway. Some people went towards their rooms. Others to the day room. I spent a lot of time in the day room. With it's blue tile floor and institutional chairs it was not exactly comfortable. The day room was better than doing endless yoga in my room with the homeless lady peeking around the curtain or trying to talk to the nurses. I had been at Brotman Medical Center for four days. I would be here for two more.

Who was to walk in but Angelina? The last person I expected to see there. Glamorous even in sweatshirt and leggings. She stood in the hallway finishing her intake. She wore thick eyeliner. Her brown hair worn loose with one long track left of what must have once been hair extensions.

I was completely dumbfounded.

The muscle relaxers and Neurontin still ran through my body. Every three to four hours the nurses took us aside for medication. Detox meds. Bipolar and Schizophrenic stuff. Vitamins. Sedatives.

I detoxed off of Ativan as well as alcohol. I was afraid of what life would be like without my benzodiazepine buffer. My shield from the world. I would be naked. Exposed. I would have to face disappointment and sadness.

But: Angelina. She had certainly seen a lot of sadness since San Francisco in 2005 when I saw her last. It was 2013 now. Eight years later. As soon as the intake nurse let her go I rocketed up to her

"Hey!" I said.

"Lena! Oh my fucking GOD!"

"It's great to see you! I'd wondered what happened to you after all these years."

"Oh God! So much, so much. Mira's in jail, again. She told me to give you back your closed credit card if I ever saw you. I have it but they took my wallet when I checked in."

"Oh shit! Thanks. I'd noticed some fraud shit going down."

"Yeah, Mira got a little sloppy near the end and got busted. You weren't the only one she was leaning on. She had a lot of lines open on different credit cards."

"But you? What have you been doing in LA?"

"Well Foxy Jennifer and I have been living together for awhile. I've been getting modeling jobs. Sometimes naked modeling jobs, you know. "

"Oh, you're a model, me too," said a tall, beautiful redhead loitering by the day room. "Hi, I'm Lish."

We all shook hands.

"Oh, you have extensions too!" Lish said. "I had my hair done for a while, but shit, I just noticed when I was coming in here that most my tracks fell out. I was on a bender. I've just been going from hospital to hospital trying to find one with a detox ward that will take me in. Cedars-Sinai doesn't have a detox ward anymore. They kept me overnight and then set discharge papers on my stomach. Seriously, I was having DT's. Couldn't even walk."

"Oh my God," I said, "That sounds awful. I had DT's while driving right before I checked myself in here."

"Yeah, sounds about right." Lish said.

"Trying to get to the psychiatrist. I never made it."

"So you finally got that stuff checked out, huh?" Angelina asked.

"Yeah," I said, "I'm Bipolar and Schizophrenic. Schizoaffective, they call it. Plus anxiety and PTSD."

"Whew." She whistled between her teeth. "Well I'm glad you finally got it figured out. I'm sorry Mira and I were so shitty about it."

"I've been diagnosed as Bipolar too," said Lish, "But I don't believe it. I never take the medication they give me because I'm afraid it will make me fat."

Chapter 11 — RECOVERY

Lish's unmedicated Bipolar Disorder was to cause us many problems in the years 2013-2016 that we were best friends. Finally, I could not tolerate her relapsing and let her go on her way to find other men to pay for her to drink in bars with more suitable alcoholic millennial shitshows as she seemed to want to do.

Lish found a more suitable partner in crime almost immediately. I saw her post on Facebook about "falling in love with" a homeless model with a motorcycle whose dog was her service dog's new best friend. Instead of jealousy a sense of profound relief and happiness filled me that she found someone more her speed.

I didn't want to hurt Lish more than I already had summer 2016 by revoking my friendship. Perhaps she was sick of me as well.

Lish could just mail me the $110 she owed me. She never did.

I texted her that I would take my cat to Maren's for the fumigation instead and not trouble her further.

Lish and I quickly cut ties and moved on. So did Bobby and I. I was so relieved that neither of them showed up at my place. I tried to live a healthier life. Quietly went about my sober industrious way on the East Side. I had no interest in trying to recapture my twenties or my thirties. I knew I was almost forty in 2016. It was time to grow up.

Lish was rail-thin in Brotman Medical center in 2013. Angelina was too. She always was super-thin.

I was puffy from boozing. I weighed 148 lbs in 2013. I weighed 104 in 2016.

"Are you detoxing off of heroin?" I asked Angelina.

"Yeah, and alcohol. I was drinking a lot. Shooting a lot. I would go to meetings, but it's like, fuck, you know?"

Angelina and I exchanged numbers. Decided we would try to stay in contact. We never called each other on the outside as we started new sober lives.

People pass through our lives and disappear. Especially people you meet in institutions because they so often are in and out of institutions.

I introduced Angelina and Lish to Greg. Greg was so excited to meet more pretty girls that I didn't hear much from him for the rest of my stay. That was fine, though. I was happy that he and Lish were friendly. I didn't need any more dangerous men following me around.

Lish collected dangerous men like the skull scarves she draped diaphanously around her high-cheekbone face in her Westwood apartment in 2016.

Lish draped a skull scarf around my neck. Put eyeliner, contouring and rose gloss on my lips. Took Instagrams that she laboriously photo edited and texted to me. I put them on Facebook and Twitter.

I followed Lish via lyfts I paid for to bars where we with flirted with bros who bought her beer and me energy drinks. Lish would sometimes sleep with these fleeting addict men. I never slept with them because I didn't want to tell anyone I had herpes.

Was the thrill worth being in Lish' Instagrams? The danger worth the way it made me feel alive once more? I'll never know. All I know is that for a brief month of March 2016 when I was broken up with Bobby I once more traipsed along the dangerous edges of there territory I knew so well in San Francisco. Yet this time I stayed sober. Celibate. Didn't get raped. Escaped unscathed.

I knew unscathed wouldn't last. I knew that if I ever slipped just once and drank or used again I would fall down the treacherous downward spiral that had so consumed me in San Francisco.

In August 2016 I told Lish I didn't want to go to bars with her anymore. Buying beers for someone I had met in Detox and Rehab was enabling her relapse. Whatever thills girl-ing out and getting dressed up with her held for me they weren't worth the very real danger of being two attractive women on the street at two am when the bar closed talking to random men.

I had no desire to repeat the mistakes on my twenties now that I was forty. I had no interest.

My best friend from Detox seemed determined with a death wish outlasting Angelina's, Brady's, Lucas' or even my own to live as if there was no tomorrow. Lish knew with her multiple terminal illnesses that she only had three to five years left to live. What she did now to have fun did not matter.

I knew I was going to live. I had to live. I had to care. I had to make responsible choices.

I was in detox for six days in March 2013. It changed me. I got sober. I got off Ativan and alcohol. I realized the compassion and humanity in a diverse range of people.

Along with Lish who was to become my new best friend for three years in sobriety, I was admitted to an outpatient rehab called Twin Town that would save my life.

I got out of detox the morning of March 26, 2013. That afternoon I had my intake for outpatient rehab at Twin Town Treatment Center.

I looked up and down the crowded West Hollywood Street for the address on Santa Monica Blvd. Finally, I realized it had to be upstairs. That or the address simply didn't exist. I searched the strip mall until I found a small elevator.

I went up. On the second floor of the strip mall there was a smooth grey opaque window that said Relapse Prevention Services with disembodied wings. I felt like angels were rising out and pulling me out to this place. I didn't believe in God, never had. But the grey glass and the door led me forwards.

I went in. There was a circle of chairs in a white-walled room. AA's 12 steps and 12 traditions hung on the wall. A patio with benches and ashtrays.

A stylish blonde woman with a boob job and expensive jewelry greeted me. She was the counselor. I felt instantly safer around her.

The air-conditioned room was loud with questions. I felt like I kept talking. Kept coming up with more and more problems. Issues. Worries. The intake went on and on. I told her all about my childhood. Adolescence. Young adulthood. My marriage. My years of addiction and alcoholism.

The counselor listened sympathetically. Took copious notes.

I felt witnessed. Felt like I would be helped. Finally, I was admitted.

I was to come six nights a week for three hours, for the first three weeks. Then two nights a week for two months. Then one night a week for the remaining two months. It was a long program. Hopefully it would work and get me sober.

When I first got out of detox I was afraid to be in my apartment with the liquor store beckoning from the corner. I was afraid I would just stroll over and buy a bottle. I needed something to occupy my time. Rehab filled it.

Every night I drove to West Hollywood. Sat in a circle of folding chairs. We had group therapy. Talked about emotions and experiences with a group of addicts and alcoholics. They were friendly and open about their lives. We processed together. Bit by bit, I came to know peace.

In the third hour we went over a handout or saw a video: the educational portion. I learned about relapse prevention. Boundaries.

Communication skills. Anger. Learned about facets of addiction that would affect my recovery.

I met a lot of other members of the group therapy group through Twin Town. I gradually became friends with some of them. Companionable with others. We shared so much of ourselves in that circle of chairs. Revealing our problems and struggles with addiction in various forms.

One of the people I met was Vick. He was a slender pockmarked gay man who wore neat suits to Twin Town because he worked at a bank. I just assumed he was gay, not bisexual. Took him under my wing as I had Omar. Started having coffee with him after group until he asked me out on a date.

I realized Vick was bisexual like myself. He was into me. Responding to my friendship with sweet romantic interest. I was just really clueless.

Vick did text me an awful lot, but I was completely convinced he was gay. I just texted back the same way I did with all my other gay male friends.

Those sneaky bisexuals. Like me.

I already had a boyfriend so I turned Vick down. I was dating Bobby by then.

Vick and I drifted after Twin Town. I wish him well. I am thankful for his friendship at a difficult point in my life.

Rehab was a drastic lifestyle change. For the first month, I was busy every single night. I couldn't attend any art events or parties with Stephen and my other friends. I just drove back and forth down Santa Monica Blvd from my apartment in East Hollywood to my rehab in West Hollywood. Six pm to nine pm every night plus travel time.

I came home and watched *RuPaul's Drag Race* related YouTube videos. I didn't socialize much except on Sunday, my one day off. My social outlet began to be rehab and the bonds I was building there.

Vanessa was a girl I met right before I stopped going after seven months. She was a beautiful stripper who I met on her first day. We would sit in the Coffee Bean and Tea Leaf under the rehab and talk. I quickly learned that she was on parole. Had been roofed at a club. Was funny as hell. I was transfixed by her exotic eyeliner-ed beauty.

I gave her my number but she never called.

I never saw Vanessa again after I left Twin Town.

I began to attend AA meetings. Haltingly at first and then enthusiastically. It was awkward. Always awkward, even with beautiful Lish beckoning me forwards into the Log Cabin in West Hollywood. AA Meetings were something social to do in the absence of drugs and drinking.

Lish and I attended AA meetings together. I learned that everyone had a story. Had a struggle. That my struggles were not the only suffering in the world. I found this obscurely comforting.

After a while the writer in me began to relish the unburdening of the soul that came with listening to the shares. Poor people therapy. Simply having a room full of people bear witness. I found the ritual comforting.

Slowly, I began to put my life back together. Slowly, I began to find joy in things again. It was a process of slowly finding my feet.

I went to a lot of AA meetings at Café Tropical. There was one every Friday morning at 10:30 am that I would go to with my long black hair extensions hanging around me. Café Tropical had meetings throughout the week. Throughout the day. So many AA and NA and CA and SXA meetings. I just went to AA.

I went to a lot of AA for a year in 2013. Before I stopped. Before I found a better safer way.

Colorful paper maché balloons bobbled from the ceiling in Café Tropical over low couches and plastic chairs. Fellow alcoholics passed a plate of pastries.

While they read the twelve traditions I noticed Foxy Jennifer in the group. She was the same. A little older. Kohl-rimmed eyes. Gold lip-gloss. I wondered if she would be unhappy to see me. I wondered if she would remember me at all.

When the serenity prayer was said and court cards were signed, I awkwardly sidled up to her.

"Um... Hi?" I said. "I don't know if you remember me. I was one of Angelina's friends."

"Yeah, I remember you. You were the one with the really short hair. Longer now. It looks good."

My hair was a lot longer. I had hair extensions, encouraged by Lish and Winona's hair. Lish went with me me to the Hair Store and her Beverly Hills salon to show me the ropes.

My model bestie was my fashion muse. She taught me about bronzer and eyeliner. She spent more money then she could afford but so did I at this phase in my life. Until 2016 when I realized I had to stop if I wanted to stay in LA.

My hair was thick in 2013. Black. To my waist.

"Thanks," I replied to Jennifer. "Yeah, I saw you and I wanted to say hi. I know things got crazy back then but..."

"Hey, it's ok. That was the past. We all deserve to start over. Listen, do you have a sponsor yet?"

"No." I only just started to work the program. I was pretty shy about stuff like this.

"Here, let me give you my number." Jennifer said. I pulled out my phone. "Call me every day. I want to hear how you're doing. We'll find someone take you through the steps. You'll see. Things will get better."

I thanked her. Went on my way. Walked the long uneven concrete sidewalk marked by broken abandoned televisions up the Silver Lake street to my car.

I never called. I was too shy. I wasn't sure if I wanted to revisit Foxy Jennifer and Angelina. Invite them back into my life although I knew they were in Los Angeles now in 2013 too.

Old using friends sounded like trouble. I learned in rehab about avoiding triggers and using people. I was afraid that my old drug buddies would trigger me. So afraid I rejected their friendship when offered.

I had to protect my sobriety above all other things.

I knew Billy Vegas moved to Los Angeles from San Francisco too. Facebook told me. He was DJ-ing around. Billy would invite me to his bands shows on Facebook. I never went because I doubted he was sober. I couldn't have using people in my life if I wanted to stay sober.

I never called anyone in AA who gave me their number hardly. I was not very social in AA. I was just too awkward and delicate in my sobriety to talk to anyone. That probably protected me from even more dangerous friends.

I barely knew who I was anymore. I was't writing or painting. I didn't know who this new person was yet. I didn't have an identity if I wasn't a writer or artist. Who was I?

"My name is Lena Cosentino and I'm an alcoholic."That was the first line of *Jet Set Desolate*. AA told me that was all that I was.

I was full of shame that I would share in the AA meetings. Slink out quietly when it was over without talking to anyone. Humiliated.

People from AA called me sometimes. One girl who called me and who I called back went by Killer. A mouthy bisexual blonde. She never told me her real name. Killer was a friend of my sponsor, Chuckles. That was not her real name either.

I met Chuckles when she spoke at Hollywood Late Night at the AT Center. During my first stint at AA when I was still married. She was my sponsor very briefly when I was trying to get sober in 2012. I relapsed. My wife died.

Now that I was sober again, I tried calling up Chuckles. Luckily, she talked to me. She invited me to the midnight meeting that she was Secretary of.

I went to Hollywood Late Night to see Chuckles. Tried to get her to sponsor me again. At first she wasn't sure if she could take on the responsibility because of her chronic PMS. Chuckles had me call her every day. She eventually decided to sponsor me.

My new sponsor was a former stripper. She wore her makeup thick. Chuckles got the moniker when she worked at Jumbo's Clown Room. Currently she worked at LACC as a P.E. Assistant. My new one-bedroom was across from LACC so I would walk down to her office weekly to meet.

Chuckles picked me up one day in her ramshackle VW with magnetic letters on it. She took me and Killer to an occult store. We smelled scented oils for a long time. Browsed in a candy store. It was fun. A nice break.

I got in a fight with my boyfriend that day. Needed to get out of the house.

Killer had me laughing as the three of us went to AA meetings together. Chuckles would inevitably fall asleep or put on makeup. I liked Killer and Chuckles. They were fun. In the friend drought that Katie's death and my rehab had produced, they were my friends.

I so appreciated the time that Chuckles took to meet with me and take my phone calls. I knew she didn't have to do this but was choosing to out of the alcoholic generosity of her heart.

Having a sponsor was like having a therapist. But when my forth step resentment list recovered too many scary PTSD-laden memories I realized I needed to get a professional therapist.

My rehab recommend one. My new therapist, Dr. Rachel Toles, was the answer to my prayers. She was slightly younger than me yet impossibly wise. Thin. Beautiful with long dark hair. She understand the writer's struggle. Schizophrenia. Witchcraft. Queer lifestyles. Pretty girl problems. I saw her for the next three years and counting. She took Medicare. Our weekly sessions had an $18 copay that I could afford. Dr. Toles guided me from misery to happiness.

I paid Rachel Toles to listen to my problems weekly for an hour. With appropriate boundaries and confidentiality it was an extraordinarily beneficial transactional relationship. I needed a therapist more than a friend by this point. Dr. Toles lasted longer then my many friends and relationships.

With proper psychiatric care I began to heal slowly from the wounds of my past.

Chapter 12 — LISH, WINONA AND BOBBY

Redheaded model Lish and I spent a lot of time together that summer 2013 until summer 2016. I moved down to three nights in rehab a week by the second month. Had more time to hang out.

Lish moved in with a girl from our rehab, Winona. She was a constant manic jangle of jewelry and scandal. Hanging out with the two of them was an exquisite train wreck of hair extensions and lurid tales. It felt glamorous. Might have been the pink cloud.

Both Winona and Lish were irresponsible unstable millennials with rich parents who funded their lavish Los Angeles lifestyles. I enjoyed them for a time. Eventually realized their toxicity and un-sustainability. Had to draw away.

One night after an AA meeting, Lish and Winona and I went to Swingers. I drove, as Lish didn't have a car. Lish had too many DUIs. She took Uber to her modeling gigs.

Lish was being stalked by a dangerous man. She had a detective with the LAPD working on it. Her life seemed lived on the knife's edge of danger and fame.

I was fascinated by Lish. Until I had heard all of her stories a million times. Could not listen any more.

Lish and I sat in the back of the diner with Winona and a couple of other people from AA in 2013. Everyone rapidly texted on their phones throughout the meal.

Lish ordered only a single large chocolate chip cookie. She was anorexic. She ate only cookies. Coffee drinks. Tea lattes. Diet cokes.

Cigarettes. It was years of friendship later that I finally saw her eat anything.

I ate Huevos Rancheros. Watched Winona wolf down nachos.

Afterwards I stood outside Swingers. Made small talk with a group of sober people whose names I don't remember. I held Lish's coat for an embarrassingly long time when she went to use the bathroom.

Lish was one of those best friends who I would do anything for. Who I loved as unreservedly and platonically as I loved my last BFF Rachel. We poured our hearts out to each other over the phone from 2013-2016.

Winona was a heroin addict who went to twenty-six rehabs in a year. Was thrown out of all of them. Tall. Slender to the point of drugged out emaciation. Long white blond and lavender extensions. Big eyes rimmed with glitter. I was extremely attracted to her.

I knew Winona was bisexual. She had had a serious girlfriend in and out of prison. But the more I learned about Winona, as we sat in that circle of chair in rehab three times a week, the more I realized she was trouble with a capital T.

Mira-level trouble. Another con artist.

Winona had a way of seeming so passionate. Empathetic. Connecting with me. Then I would realize that she had stolen something or was running a con on the edge of the charismatic chatter. It was usually a con on someone else.

Winona was a scary motherfucker. So was Lish but I didn't realize it until much later.

I had been through all this before with Mira. I put up a lot of boundaries with Winona so that nothing bad ever happened between us. Winona never came over to my house or my boyfriend's. I knew she would steal from us as she stole everywhere we went together. I had no illusions that she would treat me any differently then she treated the world.

I saw Winona at Twin Town. She talked about losing her job as a fashion rep because she went to Burning Man. Having to become a stripper to support herself. Getting evicted. This boyfriend and that one. So much partying.

I Facebook and Instagram-stalked Winona. Fascinated by her beauty and fashion sense but sensing intrinsically the very real danger she was in and that I would be in too if I got too mixed up with her. Often she wore something scanty that unveiled a tattoo on the back of her thigh or on the top of a platform shoe. I would be struck silent by her beauty once again.

These mysterious women who I have known. I am always fascinated by them. Winona reminded me of Angelina. Vanessa. Toxic praline junkie addict strippers I have known. Beautiful long-haired vampires who I knew intrinsically after Angelina not to let into my life.

‘Toxic needy love. The easily exploitable love of a queer woman for a straight woman is painful. It happened enough with Lish.

Is that the nature of a queer woman's friendship with a straight woman?

But my friend Maren the ex-model video vixen was stable in my life since we were fifteen together at La Jolla High. We went to college together at Reed. She introduced me to Bobby. Maren remained nontoxic and in my life after the shitshow of August 2016.

What preserved Maren and I for so many years is we both had good boundaries and respected each other. Once we reunited in Los Angeles and she was married to River I accepted that off-limits-ness implicitly. I respect the sanctity of marriage. I would prefer not to have sex with my friends anyway. I have learned the hard way that it just fucks things up.

Killer asked me, "the lesbian question," once when she was newly single in 2014. I turned her down because I was with Bobby. I didn't want to cheat. When you're queer, girls definitely count as cheating.

I didn't have sex with Killer, Lish or Maren. Only Killer was queer. Lish was vaguely bicurious but only with other models. Killer was the only one interested in having sex with me. But I was otherwise entangled with Bobby.

Polyamory was over for me by that point. STDs made it an impossibility. I didn't want to give my dear friends my herpes. I really didn't want any drama. Drama wasn't worth the fleeting pleasures of sex anymore.

Although favors were granted, vacations were taken and gifts were given between Maren and I as happens in close friendship they were reciprocal. We mostly hung out at each other's houses. Texted late into the night.

Maren was another well-educated woman from a wealthy family with no job pursuing an artist's life Los Angeles. Hoping for the best as I did. As Lish did. As Winona did. As Killer did.

Maren and I had had a fleeting lesbian encounter in college. She asked me if I would be willing to help her experiment. She brought over a bottle of cabaret to my red-painted Dustbin room. I showed her what little I knew then of how to please a woman on my mattress on the floor. I remember her long pale soft neck under the blue light of my sculptures.

I immediately accepted that Maren was actually straight when she told me that the next morning. Her cold soft skin had been unresponsive.

Maren and I went right back to being friends again. We never spoke of it again. Such things happen in college between friends.

That was usually the way with my diverting adventures with bi-curious friends. We went there once then never again. I didn't mind when I was young. As I got older I lost interest in the potential risk to the friendship.

After a while things in summer 2013 things got bad between Winona and Lish. They met one Saturday afternoon at Twin Town. We all had lunch at Tender Greens. Winona offered Lish the room. I knew them moving in together was a bad idea.

Lish was a model. Wealthy. Slightly naïve. Effortlessly magnetic. Vulnerable. Winona offered her the room after they just met in rehab that morning session. Winona was a former heroin addict. In her leather jacket and black thigh-highs she spun a mythical sober house lie to tell Lish's mother. Winona didn't seem like the most ethical person.

I knew Lish moving in with Winona was a bad idea but I was afraid to tell Lish this. Lish thought it was a really good idea. She really needed a place to move pronto as she was being stalked at her old Beverly Hills residence. Someone who attended the same rehab, lived close and promised rides, friends and fun seemed like the answer to her prayers.

I didn't have a good enough reason to tell Lish not to move in with Winona. So she did.

It was like Angelina and Mira all over again except trying to be sober this time nine years later. This time I was the sober one, much like then I was the one with the job. Not that I was always either one of those things or thought I was a better person. No, not at all. I was like Winona and Lish for a while, only older. Much as I had been like Angelina and Mira before.

Before I grew up.

We all struggle differently. I appreciate my friends for their important part in my life. I honor their memory by writing about them. I loved them for a time but cannot any longer except in memory and prose.

Once in 2013 I rode in Winona's car while she drove recklessly to Melrose from their place. She played Tyga's "Molly" loud in the car slapping her hand against the car door out the open window as she drove.

Soon I would visit Lish and hear that Winona was using heroin again. She stole Lish's Norco. Stole her Oxycodone for the back injured by a boyfriend in Milan. Stole Lish's Klonopin for her anxiety. Left her with no medication. Being accused by a psychiatrist whose office I visited with her of abusing her medications as they were substances of abuse for some.

Lish changed to the day program to carpool with Winona. Winona changed from the morning program to the evening program with me at Twin Town.

Lish was accused by the Twin Town staff of having a bad attitude. Lectured. When she subsequently fainted in their office they kicked her out of rehab. Lish liked to shuffle around putting on bronzer and cream blush from a Too Faced contouring palette and texting people during group therapy. The Twin Town counselor didn't like that.

So I would visit Lish in the afternoon at the big white house she and Winona shared off of La Brea after she was kicked out of rehab. Lish was kicked out of a lot of rehabs for being too sick to be there.

By 2016 Lish was diagnosed with multiple terminal illnesses. Dying slowly of Neuro-Beçhets, Lupus, Cancer, Von Willebrands, POTS and unmedicated reckless Bipolar Disorder in a Westwood one-bedroom where I visited her for eight months when she moved back to LA from Walnut Creek.

August 2016 I couldn't take Lish's lack of boundaries and dangerous lifestyle any more. Cut her lose from my life. Left her to die with my undying love, a collage of her modeling photos that hung on her wall, some Benefit Do the Hoola liquid bronzer and signed copy of *Jet Set Desolate*.

I had to leave Lish to save myself.

Of course it hurts. It always does.

In 2013 Lish and I sat in the backyard wicker chairs as she smoked endless cigarettes. Lish told me all about her boyfriend: a lawyer who really wanted to date a model.

Lish and I went to The Coffee Bean and Tea Leaf. Buffalo Exchange. The West Hollywood Recovery Center for meetings. We were always going to AA meetings. Winona would be at the West Hollywood meetings with her vast shadowy network of friends and accomplices met through the recovery system. In LA the recovery system was an industry and it's own trap.

Back when I still hoped and thought that AA would keep me sober.

I stayed sober for nine months that time. Until a single-night relapse in late 2013 prompted more by a desire to get stoned wth Alex then anything else. I smoked weed with my old friend Alex from my marriage who I had always loved to smoke weed with. I felt like I had to drink the next morning just to get the full mileage out of my relapse if I was to be relapsing. While I enjoyed the weed, I didn't enjoy the drinking. I called my boyfriend to confess in maudlin dribble. I was ashamed.

Drinking wasn't fun anymore. It was time to stop for good.

Oh yes, this boyfriend. I had a boyfriend. Spring 2013 I met Bobby Mendez. A month later we started dating.

I wasn't done mourning Katie. Quite the contrary. I needed someone living in my life also. Bobby was a good man. I fell in love with him pretty quickly.

Bobby Mendez. The summer of love of 2013. Daft Punk's "Get Lucky" always seemed to be playing that summer.

Maren and River took me hiking eight months after Katie died. I was twenty days newly sober. They brought along their friend Bobby.

He had two little dogs. Told stories about being a heroin addict in the eighties. I noticed interesting tattoos under his shirt.

I was surprised to be noticing things again. I was surprised to be noticing Bobby. He gave the dogs water in portable canvas bowls. Expressed sympathy over my wife.

We were at the helicopter pad at the crest of the trail over Griffith Park. The city in the distance. Bobby seemed so sincere. I felt sad to still be so deep in mourning. Twenty days sober. So raw. Such a mess. I could never date again, I was sure. So much had happened to me. I felt overpowered by my past. Haunted.

We began to hike downhill. The prospect of getting food and watching *Game of Thrones* at Bobby's was brought up. I ended up coming along.

I was surprised by how clean and homey Bobby's little back house in Glendale was unlike the bare mattresses in basements of the boys I'd dated before. He seemed like a normal adult. I had never dated an adult man, I realized.

Bobby was older than Maren, River and I. 49 years old. I was 37. I had never dated someone that much older then me. He was handsome. Craggy. Latino. Had a tattoo of a tiger running down one shoulder. Tattoos of skulls on the other shoulder. So many tattoos from the eighties. He said he regretted the tattoos but they looked great on his bulging muscles.

I was confused by what was stirring. I didn't really know what to do with this. When Maren, River and I went to leave I thought about what it would be like to stay with him in that cozy house.

I saw Bobby again the next few weekends. Bobby was River's best friend at the time. Maren and I recently reconnected after being friends in high school and college. The four of us hiked or watched HBO at Bobby's house.

I wasn't sure what to do with my emotions.

Katie died eight months ago. I wasn't sure if I was over it or ever would be. But I did have a crush on Bobby.

I added him on Facebook. I checked my Facebook multiple times that week. He didn't add me back. I felt ashamed but I also felt like I had to move on. My sobriety was giving me courage to live again.

That weekend, Maren and River were out of town. Bobby added me back on Facebook.

Bobby Facebook chatted with me. I chatted back. We ended up going out to dinner. I realized I was on a date when he picked me up. Walked up to my Hollywood apartment gate where I stood in my black and white striped sweater-dress. My black extensions hanging around me.

Bobby took me to a nice Mexican restaurant and paid. It was a new feeling to be on a date. It had been many years.

I was excited. We made small talk then ended up talking about drug addiction and rehab. Bobby used to be a drug addict also. It made me feel like less of an alien to share that with someone. He was sober from heroin for twenty-one years. He left AA five years ago. Started drinking lightly again.

Bobby drank a margarita with dinner. I had iced water with ceviche. He paid so I felt like I was on a date.

My medication worked a lot better since I got sober. I hadn't heard any voices for awhile. Still, I held back about talking about my mental illness until the next morning.

But that night. We ended up back at Bobby's place watching a boxing match I pretended to be interested in. He demonstrated how a southpaw hits a right-handed person. I snuggled up.

Bobby gently took my hand. I smiled. Hoped he would kiss me. He did soon after.

Bobby later told me he was completely convinced I was a lesbian up until that point on the couch when I snuggled up to him. He didn't know I was even into guys, much less him. This time Bobby was the clueless one who didn't realize bisexuals were a thing.

Well, I made the same mistake with Vick a few months later. It's an easy mistake to make.

I hadn't been with anyone in about a year. I was so excited to make out with Bobby.

Katie stopped having sex with me completely in 2012. Only once on my birthday. I knew she had something going on with James. I allowed it and forgave her for it as she had never been with a man before. I knew I didn't have a dick and a job. I wanted so badly to save our marriage. Katie committed suicide before I could get sober. I will always regret not getting sober soon enough like so many things.

I snapped the edge of my black panties almost nude in Bobby's bed in 2013.

I said, "Because this is the first date, these stay on." Bobby and I didn't have sex that night. First date I figured. I wanted there to be a second date. It was good to have boundaries now. I learned that at Twin Town. I stayed the night though.

A few nights and much texting later, Bobby and I got together to watch the finale of *RuPaul's Drag Race*. I didn't have a TV. I was excited to find someone with a big flatscreen and cable. Bobby was excited to spend time with me.

Jinx Monsoon was crowned queen. Afterwards Bobby and I had sex for the first time.

And so it went. We spent a lot of time together after that. Going to dinner. Plays. Parties with my friends. Watching his cable, which I didn't have yet on 2013. Having BBQs in his wide grassy backyard. Taking walks with the dogs. In three weeks we were dating.

In a month I sat in my panties eating the breakfast he had fixed me. Told him I was falling in love with him. It was a speeding car I didn't want to get out of. I'm not sure if it was my new sobriety or my still recent widowhood. My emotions were raw and naked. I was falling fast and hard. So was he. We spent every weekend together.

Bobby called me every day. He began to read *Jet Set Desolate* when I gave him a signed copy. He didn't finish it until after we broke up for the final time in July 2016.

Bobby put up with my hysterical text messages. We developed an elaborate emoji language.

Bobby knew I was still going to rehab but I would spend the weekends with him in his rented Glendale back house. He had two Brussels Griffons, Chiqui and JoJo. Let me park my car in his driveway. I would come over before him to wait for him after work with his dog in my lap.

Chapter 13 – SOME LESSONS COME PAINFULLY WITH TIME

To love someone with a past that threatens to engulf them is a generous thing. I hoped for three years Bobby could overcome it. We broke up July 2016.

I severed my friendship with Lish August 2016. Two weeks after. Both Bobby and Lish had unmedicated Bipolar Disorder. Both liked to live beyond their means. I could no longer subsidize or enable this.

I was a disabled woman on government benefits who narrowly escaped poverty in 2013. 2009-2012 I was on Food Stamps. I know the very real consequences of squandering my two inheritances by having too much fun with Lish and Bobby.

I enjoyed the glamorous company of this fading ex-model and high-living television boyfriend. At the end of three years felt I could no longer do it anymore. I was unwilling to be driven back to my parents house once again for being too generous with my friends as I had with Angelina, Mira, Billy Vegas, Lucas and Brady.

In the end I decided that the danger that Lish and Bobby put me in was no longer a risk that I was willing to take.

If my selfish desire for self-preservation left me without friends or lovers, oh well. I would rather be alone in the splendor of my professionally cleaned one-bedroom with enough weed and cable TV to keep me entertained then go out to bars and meet dangerous characters anymore. Or have men buy me dinner who I had to sleep with.

Some lessons are learned painfully with time.

I needed to preserve my sobriety above all other things.

Lish moved back to Los Angeles from Walnut Creek January 2016. Began relapsing saying only having a few beers wasn't really drinking. But beer is alcohol. I knew the relapsing was the beginning of the end.

I accompanied Lish to bars for few months in spring 2016. I was the sober wing woman with lyft on her phone that always paid for the drinks. I understand I was a desirable person to go to bars with for Lish. I am an excellent wing-woman from many nights with Angelina, Mira and Limone. My skills are honed with time.

I imagine Lish still has all of those fun group selfies we took on her phone, as I do too. We had so much fun, for a time. But I had to grow up.

Lish was very hurt when I told her I couldn't pay for her to go to bars anymore. But in the end I could no longer enable her relapsing the way I had enabled Angelina's. I wasn't comfortable buying beers for someone who I met in Detox, rehab and AA.

Bars held nothing for me in 2016 but spending money I could't afford on things I didn't want to look nice for alcoholic shitshows that I had no interest in sleeping with. I was unwilling to make sacrifices to enable a lavish social life. I left bars behind.

Some lessons come painfully with time.

One night in 2013 I was in bed with Bobby. When he got up to feed the dogs I saw Katie's face on the wall. Heard her voice talking to me. I recently raised my antipsychotics. They worked very well most of the time.

I was shocked by this manifestation. I didn't know if it was my psychosis or an honest ghostly visitation. Katie said she saw what I was doing. She forgave me. She knew she had stolen herself away from me. She had taken herself irrevocably out of my life.

“I am never coming back,” Katie said.

Katie knew and I knew I had to go on. I watched the green walls. Her ghostly face. I was naked in the grey sheets. Curled in the blanket. My newly stitched hair extensions fell to my waist.

I listened as she forgave me. Katie said it was hard to watch me with Bobby but that I knew I had to do what I needed to be happy. It was good that I was happy.

Bobby came back in. Crawled in bed with me. I turned away from the face on the wall.

What could I do now? I needed to live my life.

I could hear Katie’s voice saying to me, “Turn away from the window. Turn away.”

I turned towards Bobby.

I would always listen to Katie. But I needed to turn away.

I needed to take hold of my future.

I was told not to date in early recovery as breakups often caused relapse. Of course when Bobby and I broke up in December of 2013 I relapsed almost immediately. I wasn’t able to get sober from my substances of abuse yet. Mostly alcohol but a little cocaine. A cocaine threesome at the Mondrian Hotel happened in December 2013 with my friend from Portland and her boyfriend. That was the last time I ever did coke. Never again.

I checked myself into La Encinas for a week afterwards to dry out.

“Don’t fuck it up,” as RuPaul says. I did fuck it up there for a little while.

There was a lot of fallout to that January 2014 Instagram on Facebook of José and I. José was the tattooed gangster that I met inpatient at Las Encinas. We dated for a hot second in the interim between Bobby and I breaking up. I let him move in with me for three weeks. Big mistake.

I had made the mistake before of letting itinerant alcoholics move in with me. I had to never make it again if I was to survive.

Bobby was out of work for most of 2016. In July he was two months away from having to rent out his Mount Washington home and move in with his parents. I set the strict boundary that he couldn't move in with me in my expansive one-bedroom stuffed with art, antiques, cosmetics, and wedding presents.

I had to defend my space after the mistakes of José, Kelvin, Jesse and Nick. No more boyfriends or girlfriends were ever allowed to live with me again.

I drew my lines. Held firm to my boundaries. Did not allow further cohabitations since José left in 2014.

I wanted to live alone in my one-bedroom in Hollywood until I died alone.

José went to Las Encinas regularly to meet women to move in with. He lived with his strict Mexican mom on SSI for depression. José could go to Las Encinas for free because he was an ex-con. Las Encinas provided him with a string of vulnerable women to exploit and move in with.

I was one.

I posted an Instagram of shirtless, tattooed José and I playing around with a knife on Facebook one carefree morning in January 2014. I actually unfriended one of my father's friends over that Instagram when she called me out. My father's friend shared the scandalous Instagram on Facebook. Said it was sick. In such bad taste. The photo was in bad taste I was told repeatedly.

In early 2014 I was instructed by my therapist and Las Encinas outpatient doctors to try medical marijuana as a psychiatric medication for my Bipolar Disorder, anxiety, depression and PTSD. As a harm reduction substitute for alcohol, cocaine and meth.

I was definitely willing to try it. I loved smoking weed. I had never had anything bad happen with marijuana. As long as I could stay sober from my substances of abuse it would be an improvement.

I relapsed with drinking while alcoholic benzodiazepine-addicted alcoholic José lived with me. My therapist told me I could escape the expense and discomfort of another trip to Brotman by detoxing with medical marijuana instead. That sounded a lot more attractive then an expensive institution my parents would have to pay for again where I would meet more dangerous people.

I could afford a medical marijuana card and weed on my own.

AA just wasn't really cutting it for me any more.

My best AA buddy Lish had a miscarriage in early 2014. One of many miscarriages to follow because she didn't use birth control. She was raped by one of Winona's partying friends. Again, one of many rapes. She relapsed with alcohol. Again, another relapse.

By summer 2016 I couldn't take the recovery drama anymore.

I learned the hard way that it's a bad idea to hang out with people who you meet in institutions in your sober life if you want to stay sober.

I had to protect my newfound sobriety above all other things. Drugs were already a dating and friend deal breaker. I had to make drinking around me a deal breaker too.

Lish moved in with me in 2013 when she got out of the hospital for a chaotic week. Relapsed hiding a flask of vodka on my couch. Broke up with Roland there. Had sex with some random dude all over my apartment when I was at Bobby's. Borrowed my underwear.

Finally, I had to 5150 Lish to get her out of my apartment into the hospital. It was an ordeal.

After that experience I never invited Lish to my apartment again. Even during that magical eight months in 2016 when she was living in Westwood and we were best friends. I knew I might have to call an ambulance to get her out. She was constantly in and out of emergency rooms. Lish was just so unstable.

Plus Lish didn't have a car and I did. I lived on the East side of Los Angeles and she lived on the West. It would be an expensive lyft ride for her to get out to my place. Lish was scared of dangerous, dirty East Hollywood. Public transit was far too dangerous for her with her fainting spells. So Lish just never came over again.

I sat in my clean, quiet, air-conditioned apartment August 2016. Assessed kicking Bobby and Lish unceremoniously out of my life. I felt like I had made the safe, rational choice for my ongoing survival and sustainability.

I will do what I have to do to survive.

After Lish Ubered her stuff away from my apartment in 2013 we didn't talk for a year. She moved to Walnut Creek to go to the hospital for her multiple terminal conditions. Try to sort out her life.

Angelina all over again. At least I saw the parallels between my using and sober girlfriends. Another toxic praline. Just as Angelina had returned to San Francisco and relapsed, Lish returned to Los Angeles and relapsed.

Preserving my newfound sobriety was more important then fun or friends in the end. The writing and art I devoted my life to were more important. I had to have adult priorities now that I was an adult. Turning 40 in 2016.

Once again, I had to look towards my future. I had to grow up.

In AA in 2014 I got kicked out of the AT Center by a mean dyke who didn't like me taking my Court Card out early.

I kept meeting people through AA and treatment who just wanted to move in with me. I didn't want to share my space with anyone. AA was too much of a time-suck. I wasn't getting any art or writing done. I was done with AA spring 2014. AA and institutions exposed one to a bad crowd.

I felt I was safer on my own.

So I went out to get weed on foot one sunny spring day in spring 2014. Trying the medical marijuana harm reduction path rather then the Detox and AA path.

Marijuana worked a lot better. I would so much rather smoke pot and write or paint alone in my apartment then go to anymore of those dangerous meetings.

I'm still California sober. California sober is medical mariuana and prescribed psychiatric medication only. No alcohol, cocaine or meth anymore. Ever again.

That's how I roll.

The spring epiphany of 2013 was Twin Town and sobriety. The spring epiphany of 2014 was medical marijuana and my etsy small press Lost Angelene. The spring epiphany of 2015 was buying a Macbook Pro and writing *Diary of a Hollywood Hedgewitch.* The spring epiphany of 2016 was the revelation that all of the books I had been writing were a series. Spring was a fertile if manic time for me. A time of big plans and hope.

I got a medical marijuana prescription from a storefront with a banner out front on Melrose. I walked back down the street to the dispensary: The Good Life on Melrose. A long block of LACC between it and my apartment building.

In the dispensary I filled out the paperwork. I was buzzed into a mural-lined room full of mason jars of weed. Small vials of hash. Racks of edibles. A rotating staff of friendly tattooed chicks staffed it. As the year wore on and I became a weekly visitor I recognized them as allies in my quest to get better.

Soon I was playing a different ball game with my sobriety. Staying sober by smoking weed. Getting all sorts of psychiatric health benefits out of it that helped me to function better.

Medical marijuana motivated me to expand my etsy store momentarily into a small business. Weed gave me hope again even if it was delusional. I spent a lot of pleasant evenings at home getting stoned watching movies on my new flatscreen with HBO. Writing. Doing witchcraft. I was much happier.

Chapter 14 – HARM REDUCTION

I could smoke pot alone. I usually did unless Bobby joined me. I intrinsically and wisely knew that I could endanger my so valuable below market tenancy in my dream apartment if I had loud pot parties. I couldn't afford to smoke out the neighbors repeatedly. I never opened that door. I kept up strict boundaries as I must.

After Micah coming over every night to drink my wine keeping me on a tamale budget in Golden Hill I decided I would rather not smoke pot with my neighbors even if they were interested. I have no idea if they even were because I avoided them. Let them stalk me over the Internet if they were interested as people do.

I am aware people other than me know how to use the Internet. I am aware that all that I put out there could be viewed by anyone with wi-fi. I am fine with that.

I wrote achingly honest humblebrag shitshow confessional personal essays for Entropy Magazine, Mother Should? and The Account Magazine. I tweeted every hour. I wrote a series of autobiographical fantasy novels about the first forty years of my life. I put all of my paintings, writings and press clippings on my website.

I felt I gave away enough of myself on the Internet and through my work. I was very selective about who I let into my life by the time I turned forty. No more taking in fans who showed up on my doorstep the way Kelvin had in 1998. If anyone showed up announced they were not let in.

I never answered my door. Luckily no one ever knocked except my cleaning lady. If the Jehovah's Witnesses left pamphlets the last thing they wanted to do was meet a queer witch. Would I go door to door trying to convince people to be a queer witch? No!

I preferred to keep myself contained to the Internet and the printed page and be done with it. If I had to go out and buy something or go to a medical appointment I did. Otherwise I holed myself up in Hollywood to create.

Some lessons are learned painfully with time.

I would prefer for my neighbors to indifferent strangers preoccupied with their own lives. Not come into my home or drop by unannounced. I now knew neighbors would if allowed. If I had something to offer them.

I did have a lot to offer. Yet I wasn't interested in giving any of it away.

I knew the tenuous stability I had achieved by marrying well and getting sober could easily be lost if dissipated. As could my dream apartment tenancy. I could not afford to have any more expensive friends. I learned from the mistakes of the past.

I turned the Dame Darcy tarot cards drawing the Four of Pentacles again and again. "Userer, hoarder, skinflint," read the tarot definition pamphlet. I was content in August 2016 to draw the Four of Pentacles. If by sacrificing company I could gain safety and security that was a worthy trade.

I did enough dangerous thing as it was in my writing, art, Internet presence and smoking of medical marijuana. I needed to have strict boundaries if I was going to stay safe in the future.

I resolved myself to hole up and write and paint.

I waited calmly August 2016 for the next chapter of my life to start. Wrote the ending of this book. Contentedly sat in the air conditioning sipping iced coffee typing with my cat and cockroaches.

Unlike my previous favorites cocaine or meth, marijuana did not make me feel alone or crave treacherous company. It make me see a rainbow haze. Feel that the faeries were here. Feel more creatively stimulated. Feel slightly fanciful. Relaxed. Comforted. At peace.

I had an abnormal pap smear from my HPV in spring 2014. I feared cervical cancer the way I feared HIV before. I felt even more surely that I should be smoking as much weed as possible to cure the cancer. Weed is supposed to help cure cancer.

Weed cured everything to the extent that a cure was going to happen. I would always be disabled and on SSDI. At least I could be happy and functional. Live independently. Stay sober from everything else. As long as I was very careful who I spent time with.

I would prefer to be mostly alone at this point with the way life has treated me and the people I have met.

Maren, my oldest friend since high school in *Scaffolding,* stayed in my life as Lish and Bobby exited. I begged Maren to let me bring my cat to her warehouse at 9:30 am during a cockroach fumigation. She kindly let me. I had some good friends left after the fallout of summer 2016's drastic changes.

As one chapter ends, or one book ends, another begins. I haven't written the next ones yet. Stay tuned. That's the plan.

With marijuana comfortably in my life in 2014, like a soft afghan armchair/cat combo that would always be waiting for me at home, I actually got comfortable and happy for a very long time. Weed was a lot cheaper then cocaine and alcohol. I could afford to indulge in as much as I reasonably wanted to consume without financial upset as long as I rarely shared.

I briefly had a friend in winter 2016 named Janet who would come over and smoke weed with me. It was always my weed. I was fine with that up until a point, but when she began to ask to buy weed off of me without even hanging out I realized what the friendship was really about.

I set a boundary with Janet. I wouldn't sell her weed. I knew that was illegal. I don't do that for anyone.

I know that with the way I write so publicly about my medical marijuana harm reduction requires that I observe scrupulous and exact safety boundaries with it. I never procure it for anyone else. I never drive stoned. I only smoke at home inside my apartment. Never on the beautiful lanai with chairs and twining vines behind my apartment that so beckons when I take out my trash and do my laundry. The section with the chairs is really my downstairs neighbor's apartment's backyard. know that.

I respect my neighbor's space and time. I appreciate that they respect mine. I am very busy. We're all living in Hollywood in this beautiful old cockroach-ridden apartment building that I love. From what little I know of my neighbors they are musicians, students, or have jobs. My building is all one-bedrooms so no one has kids. It's couples and single people. With the exception of the occasional electric guitar or afterparty they are quiet. Keep to themselves.

Bless them.

When my neighbors party or play guitar I nod along to the music and remember that I was young once too. I am quite content to tolerate cockroaches and occasional noise if they will leave me alone to smoke my weed and write in peace. I imagine and hope my neighbors are as busy as I am. Content to work alone in our apartments as I am.

As much joy as Micah brought to my life he was an itinerant alcoholic shitshow who led me on. I would prefer not to repeat that sort of entanglement.

I would hate for the smell of my pot or my pot smoking to every be a problem for my apartment building so I never smoked in the beautiful outdoor area. It was just not happening.

I set boundaries with my neighbors. We didn't hang out.

I set boundaries with Bobby. He couldn't move in with me nor would I marry or buy property with him.

I set boundaries with Janet. I wouldn't sell her weed.

I set boundaries with Lish. I didn't want to go to bars with her anymore unless we could go dutch. I needed her to pay me back the $110 she owed me if she was getting hair extensions and spray tans.

I have learned the hard way that if by setting a boundary you end the relationship that relationship needed to end.

Setting boundaries ended the relationships with Bobby, Janet, and Lish. I never even began relationships with my neighbors beyond cordial polite distance.

Better boundaries were necessary means to survival.

At Twin Town they told me I should find spirituality if I wanted to stay sober. After that experience with Jehovah and the Grim Reaper in the psych ward, Christianity didn't feel like the right choice for me.

I decided to become a witch. Found Wicca. Wicca was the religion of the witches. There was tons of information about Wicca on the Internet and on books I could order in Amazon. I set about my research on witchcraft, my new hobby.

In early June of 2014 I did a powerful seven-day love spell from the *Book of English Magic*. A 500-page volume that I am still working my way through. The grand tradition of things in the United Kingdom. The UK is the birthplace of Wicca. Druids. Ley Lines. King Arthur. The Holy Grail. Knights Templar.

I didn't hide being a witch at all once that I realized I was one. Once José called me out.

"I know what you are. I've seen your shit. Bruja!" José said to me in January 2014.

Witchcraft was the good José brought into my life. Along with motivating me to get my own TV and cable. Along with the relapse and messy cohabitation.

There are so many witches in Los Angeles that it felt like a good place to be one. Wicca was a fashionable religion like Scientology except less expensive. I didn't join a coven. Too cultish. After AA I was done with cults. I stayed a solitary practitioner.

I didn't know when or how much my upcoming inheritance from my Katie's death would be in spring 2014. I only know that very powerful and benevolent money and stocks were coming my way from Katie, my baby girl. Taking care of me in death as well as life. If I was smart and held onto my inheritance it could remain as a cushion between me and the dangerous outside world.

Katie Jacobson. My one true love.

Katie's parents handled everything through Well's Fargo Advisors. Her mother called me and told me about my inheritance one morning two years after my wife died. A total surprise.

I used to bank at Wells Fargo from the nineties to 2010 or so. I was essentially kicked out of Wells Fargo for going on a trip with Katie and letting my bank account accidentally get $800 overdrawn. We were traveling for five more days than originally planned. My budget was just so tight back then and hers so expansive. Katie was in the lead of what we would do. We travelled as she wanted to. Had our adventure.

We went to Ely after Reno on the loneliest road, Highway 51. Then I came home and had to change banks after paying all the money back once my Disability check came in. It was a dark time for me financially, that marriage. I never had enough money. Katie always wanted to do things that I couldn't afford to do and go dutch.

I switched banks to Comerica Bank who had fewer fees in 2010. Was never overdrawn again. Instead I gradually became well-off.

It seems strange but karmic that I would be dealing with Wells Fargo again but this time they were giving me money. I already knew it wasn't not going to be an insane amount of money, but a nice bundle of stocks.

My inheritance came in late 2014. it was $1000 cash and $34,000 in stocks. I spent the cash. Saved the stocks forever as the stock market fluctuated. I needed to hold on to them. This had to last me a long time. I needed to be careful.

A cushion, finally. I felt safer with financial security. Money could cushion one from a lot of things. I so hoped that spring as I got sober and came into money that things would finally be alright. I hoped with a desperate hope.

Witch-wear. It just happened. I could perhaps help it if I had to hold down a straight job but I was disabled so I couldn't work anymore.

I just revamped my Tumblr and called it a magazine. Sold chapbooks on etsy and called it a feminist small press. None of that made any money. Back when I was pretending to have a job in 2014. Trying to seem less pathetic.

I've since given that up. Writing and art are all that I do.

I didn't have a job from 2008 onward. My money came from my parents and my two inheritances. Grandma Virginia left me $10,000 in 2014. Disability threw in about a K a month. Because I was on SSDI not SSI I was allowed to be given money only, not earn it. I lived well off of charity.

So I wrote for free as my own form of volunteer work. Trying to entertain and give back to the society that tolerated and supported me. I loved to write and paint. That was all that I wanted to do.

By the time I was 40 I didn't have a whole lot of choices but to continue on as I was living.

With this freedom I dressed for no one but the Halloween witch within my dark little soul. Even at thirty-seven. I wore vintage. Hot Topic. American Apparel. Blackheart. Little sexy shit. Mostly always leggings. Tank tops. Lots of jewelry. I ripped off what I liked about Winona's style once I didn't see her anymore.

My hair was long and thick down my back with long black extensions and grey streaks visible here and there. Finally in late 2015 I gave up on the expense of hair extensions and got a long angled bob where I could cut the bangs myself. Lower-maintenance hair saved me a lot of money.

I went in and out of dying my white roots. Part of me wanted to just let all of my hair go Cruella DeVille white and black. I would grow out the white skunk steak until I could stand it no longer. Dye it black again. I packed my "Hair Goals," Pinterest wth photographs of women with long white hair.

Why not, this "Hot Witch" thing? I didn't mind looking like the witch I was. I keep a hot glue gun-embellished copy of Dame Darcy's *Handbook for Hot Witches* on my coffee table. Great spells and advice. Even if witchcraft was just another fantasy, delusion or hobby it was a pleasant one.

Chapter 15 – WHEN LINGERIE WAS NOT ENOUGH

I hoped Bobby enjoyed it when I came over in lingerie. Even when he said he didn't like the particular set. That particular leather buster and leather thong I wore over to his place one night in 2014?

"It's ridiculous," Bobby told me when I unveiled my new lingerie. I lay on the couch on display trying to impress him. "You're trying too hard. You're not making me horny." Bobby was very critical. My new Blackhearts ensemble was a bit of a costume, I suppose. A cheap black leather corset with gold zipper trim. I never wore lingerie over to his house again.

Bobby proposed that I could wear the bustier as a top in a club. Not that I ever went to clubs anymore in Los Angeles after the mistakes of San Francisco. I could repurpose the corset Bobby instructed me. I thought that was a good idea at the time. I appreciated the fact that he thought it wouldn't work as lingerie but it would as an acceptable top in the right situation. That felt freeing.

What was lost at me at the time but I now realize is how rude that was of Bobby to reject my attempt to buy and wear to his house new lingerie. Instead tell me I looked ridiculous. Bobby pretended to be such a nice man always buying me dinner. Inside Bobby hated me as much as he hated himself.

"If you can't love yourself, how the hell can you love someone else," says RuPaul at the end of every episode of *RuPaul's Drag Race*. Bobby could not love. Bobby always said he loved me even up until the end.

I loved too much. I loved Angelina and Lish too much. Loving too much ruined me time and time again.

I liked to dress kind of slutty as I lost weight from not drinking. It was fun except when I got harassed on my Hollywood street.

Bobby and I didn't have sex that night in 2014 at all. I lay there topless in my leather thong stained with poop on the black ribbon string. Fell into blissful slumber in his soft pale green bed next to him. The glossy black wood bedroom set that loomed low. The black bento box headboard rose over our pillows.

Many days and nights in 2014-2016 were spent at Bobby's new house in Mount Washington. Up in the hills through many winding streets. Outside, a small dirt and ground cover patch. Bobby later put sod onto the patch. Long driveway stretching up the hill. I had to drive up a pitted and broken country driveway to get to the house. It was set a little bit above the street. A big wooden deck that the previous tenant built.

'The previous owner of the house since Bobby bought it in early 2014 was single. It was a single person's house. Only big enough for one person. The previous owner was a lawyer. She was also a witch, I later learned. I felt she planted good energy in the house.

I knew the previous tenant to Bobby's house was a witch because she received the Pyramid Collection catalogue at Bobby's address still, under her name. They just kept sending it. I read it. Soon it came in my name, to Bobby's house. The witches knew.

They had great shit in the Pyramid Collection Catalogue that I had never seen before. It was adult subcultural. A little bit Hot Topic. Gothic. I liked that. Meant for or a mature woman with a global, intellectual practice. No Disney or memes. No Internet stuff. It was as if pop culture didn't exist. Just literature. Steam Punk. Etsy-like unique jewelry. All for middle-aged women.

I was now a middle-aged woman.

I had no idea where the witches were that ran this strange mail order company. I liked it immensely. Maybe it was run out of someone's house that was a witch, too, like my etsy store or the online boutiques I ordered jewelry from. That made it seem even more magical. The Pyramid Collection was a secret witches catalogue. All the witches got it.

I got emails from the Pyramid Collection after ordering *Wicca for the Solitary Practitioner*. I ordered that Cunningham book on the advice of my sister Dretta. Dretta was also a Wiccan, although she didn't full-on do spells like I did.

Wicca for the Solitary Practitioner helped me to refine my practice. Circle casting and altar tips. Instruction on ritual bathing. Robes. Selecting magic jewelry. All things that I did. Felt validated by how they were spelled out here. I learned new things. New spells. Things to augment the spells that I was already doing.

Maybe the spells were working. The money spells were. I so wanted to believe in magic. I never was sure if magic was just yet another Schizoaffective delusion. It was one I was willing to go with as it entertained me.

That night in 2014 after our fight I did a spell wishing that Bobby's temper would be calmed. That he would love me as I was.

This is an effective prayer or spell format. The spell format, from Silver RavenWolf's book:

1.Take several deep breaths

2. Attain a connection with the spirit. Visualize white light surrounding your body.

3. Expression of gratitude for several things in your life.

4. Name the list of your personal Gods that you wish to call upon

5. A primal ask, for what you want.

6. Say, "It always works, Always a blessing" and smile.

I returned to this spell format again and again after casting a circle and invoking the elements to do what I hoped was magic. I may have been just playing with my new toys but if it made me feel better and kept me sober it helped.

August 2016 I decided to revisit the spell. I held my hot coffee in my right hand. Sat on the couch nude except for my blue feather-edged bathrobe. Put my other hand into devil horns.

I closed my eyes. Took five deep yoga breaths. Felt the overwhelming bliss of spiritual connection and white light flood out of my body within my mind.

Alone in my apartment I said, "Thank you for this book I am writing and how good it is. Adonis. Aphrodite. Dionysus. Persephone. Salome. Mephistopheles. Mary Magdalene. Jesus Christ. I desire that this book, *Angelina at the Serrano*, be published by a small press. That no-one sue me. That people love it. It always works, always a blessing."

I smiled. Sipped my coffee. Felt the magic. Heard the ratatat of fireworks on the nighttime Hollywood street outside.

The Pyramid Collection was clearly not located anywhere existing as a real address.

Much as my witchcraft probably wasn't real.

Much like the two business I started in 2014 did not really exist and failed by 2015. I believed in what I was doing in the fervor of marijuana and pink cloud and tried. Failed spectacularly as I so often do.

At least I managed to get my chapbook *G(u)ilt,* Katie's chapbook *Vergangenheitsbewaltigung*, and Christopher Mulrooney's chapbook *supergrooviness* out to the reading public and out of my cabinets. Lost Angelene did some things. We put out three chapbooks in a four years. Had big plans that all failed once I realized how much it would all cost. I threw in the towel in 2015 before I lost my shirt.

Mania spawns strange passions. Writing a series of books in 2016 may be yet another. At least this is free except for the iCloud storage and website fees. At least I'm not self-publishing them. At least most of the series of books I am writing I have been working on for twenty years. making them a series was just connecting the dots on the several books I was already working on.

When in doubt, write another book. That's how I roll. All I can do is try and hope as I did before.

Bobby had two purebred dogs that were as different in personality as their black and blonde, well-groomed coats. Brussels Griffons. JoJo and Chiqui. A male and female. Best friends. BFFs. I loved his dogs like they were my own.

I've never had a dog. Only rats, cats and rabbits.

JoJo, or Joseph, had the soul of a gay black man. A teenage artist. He was shy. Sensitive. Cowered from Bobby when Bobby was mad.

"The littlest Bolshevik," Bobby and I called him. His black communist beard stuck out when Bobby held him. He had earnest, beady brown eyes. A cute little face.

Maren called JoJo "a rat-mouse!" when he sat in her lap with his spine sticking up. He was so tiny. Frail. About the size of my cat if not smaller. She's plump. If you picked him up his little paws would curve around your arm and hold you back. He was all black. Slender with good lines that I wanted to draw.

Chiqui was curly. Blonde. I envisioned her as a bubbly teenage cheerleader in all the student government.

Maren called Chiqui "The Mayor of Dog town."

Bobby called her, "The Love Dog."

Chiqui loved everyone. She lived for love from humans. She sat on my lap. Licked my face.

The dogs were the kids, because Bobby and I were not planning on having any. We liked to envision the dogs as perpetual teenagers in the summer before they left for college. Peppy and adorable. Preverbal perpetual three years olds who loved us unconditionally. Didn't see any flaws. We basked in their love. When it was time for an afternoon nap, the dogs crawled on the bed. Cuddled with us.

Bobby made sure to put the dogs out when we had sex. There are some things that the kids shouldn't see. I always knew Bobby wanted to have sex when he put the dogs out.

Bobby's house had a scrubby yard for the dogs to poop in. Lie in the dirt. Stretch in. A lawn ornament black Statue of St Francis presided. Bald. Robed. Holy over the dog poop. I knelt on the earth on sunny days when I was stoned and prayed to him. Hoped the neighbors didn't mind.

Bobby's neighbors didn't seem to mind that I smoked pot on his deck.

I tucked the perfect little MAC brush that was angled in a tight line into my makeup pouch. It could put the thick black line on just so. Perfect cats eye angles.

I wanted to have eye makeup like Kreayshawn. Amy Winehouse. Winona. What hot messes they were. I ripped off so much style from my influences.

As Matias Viegener said in class at CalArts, "Good artists borrow, great artists steal." I didn't have delusions about being a great artist but I didn't mind having influences. I never stole material objects from people or stores but I did steal ideas, lives, stories, textual strategies and fashion pointers along the way. Perhaps it was learning from others. I would like to think so.

I watched many YouTube videos on the perfect cats eye. I studied this: How to be noticed and admired.

Blood red lipstick was a must. I had Viva Glam. A black compact of four red lipsticks with a little brush. Buxom red in silver tube. So many red lips. Lash-lined gel eyeliner eyes. Blush. Highlighter. Bronzer. Extensions long on either side of my face. All false, all slight of hand. Long, pointed acrylic nails that changed shade and pattern every month in 2014.

I overdid it as usual in my mania but I didn't care. I wanted beauty. Glamour. Luxury after so much deprivation.

I finally satisfied the lust for cosmetics that Mira and Angelina birthed in me a decade ago. Was it enough? It should have been. I cut back after a while. All of that sudden luxury was finally enough.

There is such thing as enough.

I lounged around naked until right when Bobby called at five on a Thursday night in July 2014. Having not heard from Bobby all day, I already decided we weren't going to Tom Cho's homo-centric reading. I scheduled in a revising session.

I dressed very quickly that night. Ran into my bedroom. Threw together an outfit. The maxi-dress looked appropriately queen-like. I put on my crows skull necklace so it fell in the deep V. I wanted to be regal. I forgot my bra in my haste.

Bobby and I got in another fight that night. As soon as I got into his tiny yellow Smart car in my deep V maxi-dress with no bra he was on my case about it. Bobby harassed me about the lack of bra. He said I'd gained weight since 2013. Problem.

Bobby was so hard about me on how I looked. Even as much time as I spent on how I looked was not enough. The Sephora makeup. Hair extensions. Acrylic nails. Lingerie. All of it was not enough for him.

My fancy Los Angeles television boyfriend was hard to please. That was why I left him two years later.

By the time we got to Bobby's house in 2014 I didn't want to go anywhere or be seen by anyone. I just wanted to stay home and watch television with Bobby. I got social anxiety really bad at the last minute about going to the reading.

I read at homo-centric a bunch of times in 2011-2012. I felt like I should go. A lot of people who I kind of knew and wanted to become better friends with would be at Stories Books that night. It was stressful.

I couldn't face Stories again after Katie's death. Katie and I put on readings at Stories Books with our series Featherless. PTSD kept me out of Echo Park where Katie and I were once were so happy. I just couldn't go to the homo-centric reading that night in 2014. I didn't go again.

Most of the time I spent with Bobby 2013-2016 was pleasant. Sometimes it was not pleasant when Bobby got angry with me.

By summer 2016 Bobby's rage overshadowed our joy. I had to break up with him completely via text message and Facebook chat.

I went over to Bobby's August 2016 to get my stuff. He was waiting for me by the side of his house. Tattoos bulging from his white shirt. He tried to convince me to stay and talk with him.

I said, "We had a good run. Thanks for everything. But it's over. I'm unwilling to get back on this cycle again with you. Goodbye, Bobby."

I cut ties. Moved on.

As summer 2016 wore on I left Bobby's house in the middle of the night angry with him yelling at me so many times. I felt I could no longer date him and stay safe. I was always afraid Bobby would hit me. He never hit me but he yelled at me a lot. Said a lot of terrible things.

"We're passionate," Bobby mansplained to me. Safety was more important than sex after physically abusive Jess, Nick and José. I would rather be alone.

Chapter 16 —FIGHTS OF MANY SUMMERS

Another night in July 2014 Bobby and I fought. His rage filled the car. Bobby hit one hand against the other. Yelled that I was nothing and nobody. I was trying so hard to be somebody and he knew it. Bobby knew how to hit where it hurt. Another reason I finally left him. Bobby hit the steering wheel so hard he hurt his hand.

We drove home through Glendale to his house. It was like being trapped with a monster. I wanted nothing more but to get away, I barely understood what I had done. Only that I had angered him terribly. As soon as I got out of Bobby's car where he yelled at me as I left.

That night turned abruptly. Gone South with the summer sun. I needed to leave immediately. Something horrible would happen if I stayed. I knew this instinctually. Implicitly. I was so glad I had my car there and could just drive away. So glad that we didn't live together.

I wanted to live with and marry Bobby for a window of time. That window closed in 2015 during *Diary of a Hollywood Hedgewitch.*

I suggested moving in together to Bobby once or twice in 2013 when I felt especially vulnerable. He said no then. That was when he lived in the back house owned by his parents in Glendale. While we were broken up in 2014 he moved into his bachelor house in Mount Washington. We lived apart. I kept my own apartment to escape to. I could be somewhere else, safe from him. It felt like liberation.

In 2016 Bobby wanted to live with me. He was out of work for most of the year. Running out of money. I said no then I broke up with him. No more itinerant alcoholic boyfriends were ever living with me again after the lessons of Kelvin, Jesse, Nick, and José.

Bobby didn't treat me right for three years. Alternating with taking me out to dinner. Good sex. Cable TV chill time with coffee and Scrabble.

I got sick of Bobby. Broke up with him. Took him back. Finally, I had to wise up. We were trapped in a dangerous cycle of abuse. Finally, I had to break the cycle.

Bobby's temper. The nitpicking about my appearance. I didn't like it. He was always trying to improve me both in appearance and submission. Sometimes I was not up for being improved. I was not interested in making the physical changes that Bobby wanted me to make.

Bobby thought I should take some of the money I was inheriting from Katie and get dental surgery on my imperfect bottom teeth. That was a ridiculous impractical proposition. Never happened.

I needed to save money not spend it given that I was too mentally ill to work for a living.

I thought that I allocated enough to my physical appearance now at my own probably ridiculous expense. Bobby got to enjoy my appearance. He got to walk around with me with me looking like this. He didn't pay for it.

Two weekends in summer 2014 I bought Bobby lunch twice. Once a restaurant. Once at the drive through. To be nice. Show him I was grateful for him being such a nice man.

I had enough money right now, finally. I hoped it would last now that I wasn't a drug addict or alcoholic. I worried that it wouldn't.

In the past, the most abusive men who I dated were men who I was always financially supporting. Kelvin. Jesse. Nick. José. I held off paying for anything when I hung out with Bobby mostly because he always seemed to want to pay. I felt when I started paying for things the violence started. Was it a sign?

After our fight I returned home to my vortex in Hollywood. Alone with my cat in my apartment. I did the morning meditation that I ignored that morning at Bobby's

Bobby didn't like me to do witchcraft at his house. He didn't approve of my practice of Wicca at all. He didn't see it as a legitimate religious choice. The same as Judaism or Buddhism just a little more obscure.

That was how I saw Wicca. As a legitimate protected religious choice. A better hobby than drinking. Something healthier and more fun to do at night than go to bars

I wondered if Bobby's mistrust and disapproval was a result of him being raised Catholic. His parents were heavily Catholic. He was still to some degree Catholic in his soul. He wanted our imaginary child to be baptized in the Catholic Church. I absolutely vetoed that.

Bobby didn't approve of witches. So I kept the witchcraft confined to my own apartment.

No wonder sometimes I preferred being in my apartment alone. Free. Unconfined. A room of her own is so helpful to the female artist. I could write. Paint. Do witchcraft. Smoke weed when I chose.

I finally enjoyed living alone of the first time in my life. I hoped to live alone always. I wanted to die in that Hollywood apartment in fifty years after publishing a bunch more. Have the cat I would have after Nevada eat half my face before I was found weeks later. I chose my path finally at near forty. Hopefully I would be allowed to lead the life I wanted to.

The marijuana was sometimes a problem with Bobby. Not that he liked it or smoked it too much. More that he liked it less than I did. I tended to do consume marijuana quite a lot more than Bobby did. The amount that I consumed was not a problem to me.

Marijuana enhanced my life. Kept me sober from alcohol. A recreational substitute than I could turn to for the same reasons that I used to enjoy drinking. A harm reduction measure.

I also enjoyed coffee and energy drinks when I was looking for focus and endurance. Such in these long late nights of writing and revision when I chased the faerie insomnia to the outer reaches of dawn.

Marijuana helped me to feel spiritual and connected. It helped with my yoga practice. My enjoyment of visual media. Music. Sexuality both alone and with a partner. Writing. Painting.

Bobby used weed to enhance sex. That was about it. Occasionally he liked to vaporize weed. It was always an occasion when he did. Something celebratory.

I smoked pot every day. Often during the day as well as several times during the night. This was more often than Bobby really wanted to consume it.

Bobby had a demanding freelance office job during the week. A strict sleep schedule and work ethic. He woke up early. Went to work all day. He couldn't stay up all night like I could. Our lives were different in many ways.

When Bobby was out of work in 2016 he went to the gym. Watched cable. Worked on his reel and website. Sent out emails trying to get a job. He idled once his time was free.

My work ethic ended up being stricter then Bobby's in the end. When I wasn't at his house I was almost always working on one novel or essay or another. When I broke up with him I devoted myself completely to writing.

I really enjoyed staying up all night. I found that my best writing, studying and art happened at night. I liked to stay awake until sunrise. Do sun salutations and a meditation ritual at my altar at sunrise. Our different sleep patterns drove a rift between me and Bobby.

Irregular sleep patterns was a pleasure I think which dated from the period in the early millennium when I used to love to do coke all night. Watch the sun rise with Mira, Angelina and Limone in that filthy apartment on the Haight. With Brady and Lucas in that squat in the Tenderloin. I would fall asleep all day. Rise again to roam the strobe-splashed abyss of San Francisco's nightclubs.

Back in 2001-2005 when buying coke and alcohol for my friends felt worth it in exchange for company. Before CalArts crystalized me into a writer. Before I decided what really mattered and what didn't.

Much like I ruthlessly stroked on MAC Lip Glass in the Butler Building at CalArts I ruthlessly moved on with my life when I had to.

As I left Portland in 2000.

Left San Francisco in 2005.

Left San Diego in 2006.

Graduated from CalArts in 2008.

Was unwillingly widowed in 2012.

Life goes on, inexorably.

Every relationship has a lifetime. I know that by now.

I wanted only to be in my Hollywood vortex. Working always on my creative projects. I was most likely to see the sunrise that I so enjoyed if I stay up all night. I was nocturnal as much as possible from 2014 onwards. I slept all day often.

Daytime plans rarely interfered. Being totally and permanently psychiatrically disabled and having my income stream set up worked out for me as I didn't have to go to a day job. I could write all night. Finally I could do what I loved and had been educated to do full-time. Write. All I wanted to do was write.

Even with the rocky transitions and closure of severing Bobby and Lish from my life. I know that I was on the right path. Doing what I had to do to survive.

Early Monday morning in July 2014. Almost four am.

Lana Del Rey's *Tropico* flickered from the TV screen with the sound off. Nevada laid on the floor after a cuddle session. I tweeted a photograph of her. I loved to tweet all night hoping I was entertaining the other insomniacs out there in the anonymous abyss of the Internet.

The Internet fueled me. The Internet published me. The Internet validated me. The Internet allows shy reclusive me to network. The Internet allowed me to be both visible and invisible. Public and private. The Internet was a stoned Schizophrenic rainbow haze all around us. The Internet lived in San Francisco where I lived from 2000-2005.

I wanted to write love letters to the Internet. Find me there. Only there.

Nevada rested in my apartment that early Monday morning in July 2014. I felt myself invigorate as the coffee took hold. Half a cup in a tall white mug decorated with brightly colored Eskimos sat to my right. I wore a dusty rose silk housedress. Sat on a black leather Ikea desk chair. It was neither cold nor hot. It was perfectly quiet.

The coffee cup that I drank from used to be Katie's. Today was her birthday. I felt I must spend it alone in observance of her passing. The wedding ring and HATE two-finger ring that was hers sat heavy on my fingers as I typed. Being a widow I would always be haunted. I felt I could never marry again nor did I want to.

Later that morning I watched the pale fingers of dawn creep through the white curtains. A shimmer of blue. I unfolded the pink leopard print yoga mat. Commenced my sun salutations. My body cracked and popped releasing the tightness of a long writing session. I saw the sunrise when I stayed up for the sunrise.

Sun salutations to the rising sun were my favorite things to do while in detox. Rehab. A psych unit as the stay turned and I began to feel better in 2013. I would wake early. Do my morning yoga with a towel on the institutional floor. My mind body and soul open to the dawn outside the window that many times I could not usually even see at all. Opaque institutional windows.

Drinking led to "Jails, institutions and death" as they say in AA. I had seen enough of institutions. Now that I was sober I wanted to stay away from all of that.

The rising awareness of light in the institutional dawn. I turned to sunrise sun salutations again and again as a self-soothing mechanism when troubled.

Bobby claimed to let me do what I wanted and make my own decisions. When we were together he preferred that I did what he wanted. That never changed.

I smoked more pot than Bobby wished. He disapproved. Would make it difficult or problematic for me to consume it. I brought my own pot over to his house. It was one of my psychiatric medications. A very helpful one. Approved of by my therapist and Aurora Las Encinas psychiatric hospital.

Yet medical marijuana was not approved of by my past psychiatrist. Dr. Raja thought that although I did not seem to be suffering any ill effect marijuana was classified as a drug and that must make it bad. She wanted me to cut down. I cut down somewhat, then switched psychiatrists to Dr. Abad-Santos.

The doctor I saw in July 2016 about my drastic weight loss didn't say that there was anything wrong with me smoking pot every day. Weed helped a lot with the anxiety that was really hitting now that I switched from alcohol to coffee.

I smoked weed in Bobby's bathroom in 2014 with the fan on. In 2016 I smoked weed on his front deck. The rules kept changing. Bobby yelled at me if I coughed or took longer than he wanted me to take. He was very impatient. He didn't seem to realize that it took me a certain amount of time to smoke a bowl. I didn't want to just throw away my pot without smoking it properly.

I was lucky to have such small quality problems in 2016 after how bad it was in 2004. Twelve years earlier. Mira screaming at me every day because my chicken set off the fire alarm. Not having enough money for food much less alcohol or drugs. Herpes outbreaks. Selling my shoes, work clothes and CD's for drug money. Angelina slyly stealing my prized green Hole 7" of "Retard Girl" that I showed her one night to sell at Amoeba for drug money before she left town. When Angelina disappeared my black fleece hoodie with the cat ears also disappeared with her.

I was rescued by art school. Marriage. Sobriety. Growing up.

I added Angelina on Facebook one night in 2016. Discovered she had a slightly different Italian last name. Lived in Amsterdam. Ran an online magazine that seemed blog-like called Angie's Diary. I was proud of her. She became a writer like me! Her fate seemed fitting.

I knew Angelina stayed in hostels after leaving our Haight apartment in 2005. She may have met some people in one who influenced her to go to Amsterdam after I ran into her at Brotman. Angelina lived in Amsterdam now. If she was still using it must be more socially acceptable there.

I was so glad Angelina was okay. I followed the Angie's Diary Twitter. Liked it on Facebook. Never actually looked at the site almost because I almost just didn't want to know. Angelina was in the past. It's hard for me to stay mad at people for very long. Twelve years had passed. Yet I still was glad she kept her distance.

Angelina never Facebook chatted me or commented on my pictures or posts. Her profile picture was a painting of her face but I remembered her face so clearly. Her profile had two thousand some glamorous friends so it looked like she was keeping very busy. Our world had shifted in twelve years. She was across an ocean. Thus I felt safe writing a book about her.

I hope Angelina doesn't sue me like I always hope about everyone in my books. One of my biggest fears next to getting arrested or evicted for publishing something is getting sued by someone I often by writing about them. Risks of being a writer. I change enough names, I hope.

This is fiction, after all. Who would trust a crazy woman to write the truth? This isn't the truth. I'm so fucking delusional anyway as you've probably already figured out after reading this.

Please forgive me, all those who I have loved and left and write about. I leave you this book as memento as I can't hang out with you anymore.

I'm so sorry, about all of it.

Novels are the waste product of my broken life. If my novels entertain people then I am not wasting my time, for all that Bobby thought that I was.

Chapter 17 – HAPPY ALONE WITH COCKROACHES AND FEATHERS

Bobby and I went by a strict doctrine of "My house: my rules." On the rare occasions that Bobby came up to my Hollywood apartment in 2013-2016, he watched me smoke weed in my living room while watching TV with him without seeming perturbed. It happened so rarely that Bobby came over to my house but it was always so fun. He would yelp when he saw a cockroach.

A cockroach crawled up Bobby's leg July 2016 when we were making up after yet another fight. He left rather rattled.

When Bobby came over we had sex in that blue feather-edged bathrobe that I ordered from Yandy. I lounged around incessantly nude beneath that bathrobe feeling like a Hollywood starlet.

The glamour I felt in that bathrobe was worth the heaps of blue feathers that scattered on my apartment's glossy hardwood floors. I picked them up. Piled them on a mirrored boudoir tray that my ex-girlfriend Marith sent me for Christmas in 2015. The blue feathers piled. I wondered if cockroaches crawled among the pile of feathers by my head as I slept.

The cockroaches showed no special interest in the blue feathers as I would think that they would. Cockroaches and feathers littered my Hollywood apartment in 2016.

Five thirty am at the end of July 2014 I commenced morning meditation. I had everything I needed here on my altar in my apartment. Lana del Rey concert footage flickered from the television with no sound.

I was as addicted to my rituals as I had been with to drugs and alcohol. Perhaps spirituality was an effective substitute as it was proposed at Twin Town. Wicca and weed kept me sober from alcohol, cocaine and meth. That was a massive improvement.

The Hedgewitch sunrise ritual that I began to do in spring 2014 and every morning since required a few simple supplies. A glass of water. A morning beverage like coffee or tea. A white candle. A bell. I meditated indoors always. Words were spoken: affirmations, invocations.

I always felt better and more centered after I did this meditation ritual. I felt like Bobby wouldn't approve if I did the ritual with him around at his house. I didn't want to live with Bobby after a while partially because he would be against this as he was against so many other things in my life.

One of the many nights that Bobby and I fought I stayed up all night after I went home. Did yoga to the most peaceful meditation video I could find on YouTube. The video on the screen had titles in Spanish then images of candles burning quietly, digitally. The low murmuring hum of machines.

I got stoned a couple of times that night. Ate a pot cookie at dawn. I masturbated to BDSM porn until I came and was exhausted. Went to sleep around eight am.

I did everything that I know to do to sooth myself. Except drink alcohol or do street drugs. I knew that that wouldn't help. 2004 was a long time ago. A decade later I had learned safer alternatives.

I was so thankful for my California sobriety.

After such a harrowing period of meth, cocaine and alcohol addiction I found sobriety from my substances of abuse. Much more pleasant. Legitimate psychiatrist-prescribed Benzodiazepine and medical marijiuana dependence from 2014 onward was nothing to worry about in my mind. That counted as sobriety to me and to the piss test that I took at Aurora las Encinas in January 2014. Thank the Goddess and the Horned God of Wicca I wasn't drinking anymore yet I didn't have to go to those dreadful meetings anymore either.

10:30 am on Monday morning. July 21, 2014: Katie Jacobson's birthday. She was dead from suicide almost two years now. It felt so strange. I felt both distant and close to her. It was like she was all around me yet forever gone.

I tried to come to terms with it. Tried to heal from her passing to the extent that I would ever be able to. I was in love with someone new, or I had been. It felt like there was a palpable possibility that Bobby and I might be over that day in July 2014. July 2016 was finally the end.

I felt it was over so many times and so many times Bobby and I got back together.

I forgive and I am forgiven.

We were both good at forgiving. Too good. It became a damaging cycle of emotional abuse.

I forgive and I am forgiven. I hope that whoever reads this book can forgive me for my trespasses and missteps. I am aware that my readers could be everyone and anyone and no-one. I will never know who they are unless they tell me.

On July 2014 I was not as broken as I was in 2004 with the psychosis, addiction and alcoholism. But not a day went by that something didn't remind me of Katie. She died in October 2012. Her things were still all over my apartment. I touched or wore or used something that had belonged to her daily. Katie's things were now part of my possessions in my vortex in Hollywood.

I lived in that apartment alone with my cat Nevada Jacobson-Cosentino. I hoped in 2016 to live this way for the rest of my life. By my calculations I had about fifty years left until I died of old age unless an asteroid hit. Or I got run over by a bus. Or the revolution came and I was killed like Marie Antoinette.

As long as the San Francisco gentrification cancer didn't spread too far and price me out of my happy little abode. I could happily rent here until I passed away from natural causes in the heirloom four poster in the bedroom. My Schizophrenic grandfather and wife died in that bed before me. It was fitting that I die in that bed. I earmarked my corpse to be eaten by the cat I would have after Nevada. Dead alone in my apartment for a week, face eaten by my cat was a fate I aspired to.

I told my therapist about my goal. She seems amused. It's good to know what you're doing, or think that you do.

Nevada Jacobson-Cosentino was part of the remains of my union with Katie. She was a blue-grey and white cat. Plush with deep green eyes. Green eyes like her mother. Katie also had the big green eyes. Nevada accompanied me on my day of solitary remembrance. Our cat daughter. In her own way, I knew she remembered Katie. She had a little piece of Katie living on in her.

Nevada was my companion. My familiar. My friend. Nevada was in my custody after the death of one of her mommies.

Nevada wore clothes. She was a cat who was so chill, mild and well-behaved that she would wear clothes. She had a pink dog sweater that she would wear on occasion that said, "I Have Two Mommies" with two female restroom figures in hot pink on the back. I put the "Two Mommies" cat sweater on her for Katie's birthday.

I took the cat clothes out again on May 16, 2016. Maren and Geoff come over to catch up and watch the *RuPaul's Drag Race* Season 8 finale. I put the Miss Mexico cat dress on Nevada that Katie and I bought her at the Cancun airport on our honeymoon. White wife-beater material that read "Miss Mexico" in red thread above a bow and a ruffle acting as the skirt to the cat dress. I took pictures of the dressed up cat. Put them on Facebook, Instagram and Twitter.

Maren arrived at my house at nine pm via Lyft. We watched the first feed of it talking rapidly about her marriage. My Bobby go round. The isolation of writing. The joy of late nights. I fed her a cold piece of onion-red pepper-mushroom pizza that I ordered earlier that evening.

River came over to join us around midnight after we watched the first broadcast of the *Rupaul's Drag Race* Finale. We watched it again with the sound turned way down late into the night. River and I alternated packing bowls.

I gave Maren and River the serious advice that they shouldn't stop paying rent on their warehouse space just because the building had been sold. I told them on my orange flowered couch that they should instead treat their warehouse like a normal rental. Pay rent up until the time when they wouldn't be using the space anymore.

Maren and River left. I texted Maren when she got home that I hoped that I wasn't "Giving River advice like a mom." She reassured me that it was appreciated. She said she needed the girl time.

I got up from the computer two years earlier in July 2014. Got out a tiny jar of apricot jam that my mother sent me from her trip to Eastern Europe. I began to eat it with a spoon. Delicate, sweet fruity bites: sustenance. I got out a Trader Joe's tin of slightly stale Triple Ginger Snaps. A bunch of them were still left. I had been working on them for quite awhile. I began to eat them. This was about the rest of my food, but it was something. It would have to last for now until after I slept.

But when would I sleep? It was almost midday. I had been up all night. I was used to this. Sometimes I would just stay up and stay up for as long as I could. It would feel natural and right. I would just slide into the next day and go to sleep at a reasonable time in the evening. Just skip a night of sleep and the Saphris with it. Wait until it was the next logical time to sleep. Until I actually honestly was tired.

I had so much energy and unstructured time. I just wanted to write. Smoke pot. Listen to music. Paint. Take intermittent yoga breaks. Watch Lana Del Rey videos. Whatever came up next.

I still live like this is 2016. It's great.

I felt in like I could really almost go on with this all day in 2014 with perhaps an order of Thai food if I got hungry. I would put a T-shirt on over the sports bra if it came to that.

I dawdled on the page.

The YouTube video of Lana Del Rey's *Ultraviolence* full version played "Is This Happiness." Looking at Lana's flickering, sad face. In the still of the night with headphones in, I listened.

I lifted weights at dawn to Lana Del Rey. Music lulled me in a pleasurable soothed state.

The higher dose of Klonopin was working. I felt tranquil, finally.

On May 20, 2016 at 6:26 pm I read over those words in the *Angelina at the Serrano* manuscript. They remind me to take my afternoon Klonopin and Trileptal for the day. I usually took them anywhere between five pm and six pm. I picked the pink and orange pills from the blue plastic pillbox in my purse. Washed them down with black coffee that I made in Bobby's kitchen.

Bobby was at the gym. I didn't want to go hiking with him this afternoon. I wanted instead to get froyo or frappuccino's. I felt the need for rest and calories, not exercise. So Bobby went to the gym by himself. Left me at his house to edit and write, as I did.

Near the end Bobby called my novels, "useless." That was one of the meanest things he ever said to me and he said a lot of mean shit. These novels were the reason I still bothered to be alive.

Bobby never understood that my writing was more important than he was. Writing always was and always would be more important than Bobby.

Chapter 18 – PURPLE RAIN

The cold night of May 19, 2016. Lish, Lish's off again-on-again boyfriend Roland, Bobby and I met at The Normandie Club in Koreatown. I waited in the bar with Larry for an hour for Lish and Roland to show up. The delay was expected. They were coming from the West Side to the East side. Always a trek.

While we waited Bobby nursed a Manhattan. I gulped a coke out of a bottle in measured slurps from a straw in a tall glass. The bar was dim and comfortable. We sat in a leather booth until Lish and Roland showed up.

As soon as they showed up it was time to go to the screening. We walked through the pockmarked streets. Bobby and Roland up front made conversation about man-things. Lish and I caught up in the back. She was very ill. Venturing out at night with her new-for the moment boyfriend.

Lish was not sure if she would last very long with Roland. She giving it an honest try. I hoped that by Bobby and my love we could bolster Roland and Lish's.

Roland was Lish's controlling sober boyfriend that she broke up with and got back together with over and over again. Much as Bobby was for me.

Double dating

Two by two we got to the Wiltern. Teal blue and pink of the Marquee up Wilshire. We queued up in the line. A woman came by and gave each one of us a beautiful a red rose.

"A rose," she said. "For Prince," she said. I was moved. It was a beautiful gesture. Bobby gave me his rose. Roland kept his and Lish's. I held the roses in the theatre.

Lish bought a Prince T-shirt from a vendor for $10. She tried it on. Put a photo of her in it on Facebook. Lish was occupied much of the night with taking selfies in her Prince T-shirt. She put them on Facebook. Didn't tag the rest of us.

Lish took some photos of Bobby and I too. She texted them to me the next morning. I put one on Facebook with Bobby and I together. Me holding our two roses. Us looking very much in love as we were still then. I tagged Bobby and Lish but not Roland as we were not Facebook friends. I didn't feel like it was practical or wise to be Facebook friends with all of Lish's men. There were so many.

I strongly did not want Lish's dangerous men looking me up later or Facebook chatting me. They could observe me over the Internet if they so chose as I allowed everyone I used to know but that was all that I would allow.

Roland, Lish, Bobby and I walked into the lobby. There were purple projections of Prince on the walls. Roland bought he and Lish pretzels. Bobby took off with me to find seats. Went back to buy me popcorn and him a beer. We waited a long time for *Purple Rain* to start. Watched the pink curtains and Prince memorial projections. My phone died. Bobby and I played pass and play Scrabble on his iPhone for a little while.

Finally, the film began. It was all purple velvet. Motorcycles. Clubs. Darling Nikki for a while. Cinematic excess.

Finally, Lish was too sick to stay. She and Roland had to go back to the West side. We said our farewells. I got up to hug Lish awkwardly. Waved at Roland. Bobby and I went back to watching *Purple Rain*.

Bobby whispered in my ear about going to BGD Tofu house for dinner afterwards right up the street. Soon we left the Wiltern and went to the Korean diner for heaping plates of spicy pork bulgogi. Kim Chi. Hot stone rice. Little plates of pickles condiments. We ate and ate.

On the drive back to Mount Washington I asked Bobby what time it was.

"12:30," he said. It felt like bedtime.

At Bobby's house I got stoned first under a full moon on his deck. Slipped between green sheets to sleep almost immediately.

Bobby had opinions on my appearance that he told me for the three years we dated. He art directed my outfits like Kanye West with Kim Kardashian. It irritated me yet I put up with it for a time. Yet I didn't always make the changes he requested.

For a while in 2014 Bobby kept bugging me about how I should spend a few grand and get dental surgery on my bottom teeth. My teeth were perfectly fine. Perhaps one was inset a little and a little stained, but I was doing white strips. My teeth felt and worked fine. I couldn't afford nor did I want to allocate the funds on fixing my teeth to make them absolutely perfect even when my inheritance arrived from Katie.

I did not need to be perfect. I was good enough. I did enough towards my appearance in summer 2014. I spent enough on enhanced hair and nails and the gym, none of which I was doing anymore by summer 2016. I felt I looked fine. Bobby's need to have a perfect girlfriend irritated me. Sure this was LA but this was getting ridiculous. I didn't want to or have to keep up with whatever Joneses he imagined.

My teeth were never a problem until Bobby. I don't think I have ever lost an opportunity because of my teeth being slightly imperfect. My teeth were not bad. The top set was perfect. The bottom front incisors had two issues.

Greg in detox told me I had really good teeth, especially considering the sort of life that I had lived. I went through a lot of painful retainers when I was a child.

My top teeth were perfect and white. You rarely saw the base of my bottom teeth anyway where the coffee stain was. Bobby so harped on my teeth being imperfect. I was maddening.

Lish told me that if any man thought she should get dental work she would break up with them. I should have broken up with Bobby a lot sooner.

Finally in October 2014 I went to Bobby's family dentist. Got a basic cleaning and exam for $156. I was willing to pay it to get him to stop bugging me. I got my teeth fixed for Bobby. I did it twice at six month intervals then never again.

I thought it was sweet at first that Bobby wanted me to take care of myself. The dental hygienist cleaned off the brown gunk off my bottom front teeth. That was great. But the brown stains came back again and again.

Bobby bothered me about brown gunk on my teeth about every six months. In May of 2016, he asked me again if I want to go to the dentist in Encino with him.

I said, "I'll think about it." Later I say, "Yes I will go to the dentist with you."

I still hadn't gone by July 2016 when we broke up. I had books to write. My appearance became less of a priority. I didn't want to spend the money.

Bobby didn't understand how close I still felt to poverty. How easy if would be to lose everything. How I simply could not invest that kind of money on something as frivolous as my appearance.

'Paying for dental surgery out of the inheritance left by my wife? Are you fucking kidding me? No! My appearance was fundamentally not all that important anyway compared to how I felt on the inside.

I was coming out of a decade of real heart-wrenching addiction and alcoholism issues, the last thing I gave a fuck about was having perfect teeth to please my fancy perfectionist LA boyfriend. I suppose at least he didn't want me to get a boob job but that would have been inexcusable too.

How I felt on the inside did not necessarily improve at a ratio to how I looked on the outside.

In August 2014 I felt terrible but looked good. Wearing a forest green dress with a raised velvet pattern. Eating a blood-red steak at Colombo's opposite Bobby while he harped about my flawed teeth.

A week later I felt fulfilled while not looking all that great. Painting. Writing. Wearing a shapeless smock. My hair in a damp braid. Covered in Mod Podge. Drinking coffee. Conspiracy theory documentaries from the Mutual UFO Network buzzed from the TV.

It was more important to me to feel better then to look perfect. No matter how I looked I might still feel like shit. Such was the nature of my disease.

I was still very close to danger. I will always feel it. Even with Mira, Angelina, Billy Vegas, Tank, Winona, Lish and Bobby gone from my life. So many goodbyes and memories both fond and toxic. I tell myself that the changes I must make are healthy and necessary for my sobriety and financial security.

Hollywood: May 21, 2016. I lay back in my blue feather-edged bathrobe on my orange flowered couch. Typed into the Pages iCloud void of my silver macbook Pro. A cup of coffee with a Lil Miss Sunshine on it was to my right on the coffee table with my gold and white iPhone 6. I picked it up. Looked at it to see someone has pinned my pin on Pinterest. I got an email from Barry's tickets for tickets that I ignored. A motorcycle revved outside.

May 20, 2016, Bobby and I went to Historic Monument 157 to watch Maren and River's band Pet Sex and Pet Sox play. It was the definition of not my scene. I didn't like scenes anyway now that I was an adult.

After being a scenester in San Diego, Portland and San Francisco I was finally done with scenes.

These hipsters at HM 157 were too cool and Euro to want to talk to me in my plain black American Apparel leggings. Slinking around in my owl sweater. Cropped leather jacket. Black and red leather scarf from Ecuador. Every girl at HM 157 was in a dress and heels. I felt out of place. I was wearing leggings as pants with a sweater. My slender 105 lb body wavered as we moved from the living room to the back yard again and again awkwardly.

Maren texted me that Pet Sex went on at nine pm. Bobby and I showed up at nine. We sat on a maroon sectional in the backyard under the full moon. Projections of Yan Svankmeyer animations and Merrie Melodies skeleton danced on the wall ahead where a band set up. Small tables with chairs and candles were scattered around the backyard. A bar stood to the left by the back of the house. One of Maren's friends from Spain sold sandwiches at a table next to the bar.

I texted Maren, "We're here! Where are you guys?"

Maren texted back, "On r way. R is having a manly anger fit, as befits him."

I texted, "Oh dear, I'm sorry."

Maren texted, "I promise show'll still b fun and not go 2 l8."

I texted, "Ok. We're just here, feeling like we're here very early. What's R mad about?"

Maren texted, "Make yrslf comfo, maybe find a sectional. Poop emoji. R almost always gets mad right before shows, moving equipment and being n a hurry/l8. It's like 'Dad' anger."

I texted, "Oh dear. We are in a sectional already in fact."

Bobby and I talked awkwardly on the couch in the backyard of Historic Monument 157 under the full moon. I considered asking him if he wanted to play Scrabble on our phones to pass the time as we did in The Normandie Club the night before. I didn't because I thought it would seem too antisocial. Bobby got up and made small talk with the German bartender. Got a glass of red wine.

Maren texted me, “Ok, we’z here. Loading n. We play nside, I think. I’m wearing some o lipstix u gave me “ I gave Maren a Sephora Kat Von D lipstick set for her birthday last year. I loved to give my girlfriends fancy makeup as holiday gifts now that I could afford to.

I texted, “Oh cool!! We’ll come inside then.”

Maren texted, “U’ll get 2 meet Cousin Melody. She luvs lana d r, 2.” Melody was Maren’s husband River’s best friend who she suspected he was having an affair with. A lot of people loved Lana Del Rey. It wasn’t enough to get me to be friends with someone who was tearing my oldest friend’s marriage apart.

I gathered Bobby. We walked up the back steps into the living room and sat down on a couch. It was a cold May night. I was freezing.

I texted Maren, “Oh cool. We’re inside.”

Bobby and I watched as River came in with a girl who was not his wife but looked very much like his wife. We watch him unload band equipment with her.

Bobby turned to me. “Is that Melody?” he said. “The best friend? Uh oh.”

“I know, right,” I said.

That night in a hot hot bath with Bobby I crept in close. Embraced him. Nude.

“Let’s never get married so that we don’t have to get divorced,” I said to him.

I was so glad I never did marry or divorce Bobby because that’s what would have happened had we continued upon that path. Sometimes one has to break the cycle of abuse.

Chapter 19 — ROSE-SCENTED BLANKET FORT

May 21, 2016. I sat at my computer. Looked at the *Angelina at the Serrano* manuscript.

Maren and I texted back and forth about her coming over. What she was going to do about this problem in her marriage. She said she was going to get groceries, then come over.

I sat and waited for Maren drinking coffee. I wore my blue tweed cold-weather leggings that Bobby gave me and the owl sweater. It was a cold May. I was emaciated.

I had no food in the fridge. I considered ordering a pizza again. All I ate that day was half a bran muffin and a Venti Caramel Cone Frappuccino from the drive-through Starbucks in Eagle Rock on the way home from Bobby's. I got a frappuccino instead of stopping at Trader Joe's to get groceries. I hated the grocery store but I needed food.

Lish, Bobby and my therapist were worried I was anorexic in spring of 2016. I thought I might be. My thinness might be the result of not drinking, aging and doing yoga as I did every morning.

July 2016 I went to a doctor who told me the weigh loss was my thyroid. I decided untreated hyperthyroidism was a luxury problem I didn't mind having. Resolved to love my underweight body. Stocked up on ice cream. Continued doing strenuous yoga. Decided that if anyone felt uncomfortable about how thin I was it was no longer my problem.

As with so many things, I couldn't afford to care.

Through the walls of my Hollywood apartment I could hear my neighbor singing bravely on May 21, 2016. It gave me courage.

I texted Maren, "Marriage is so hard. I'm like averse to trying it again which Larry hates but has to live with. But you are married so you are caught in the belly of the beast trying to work it out. Sounds like a good time to assess your options. What could you do about this and what do you want to do about this. I heartily agree that not wanting to make any drastic moves is a good choice."

Maren texted back, "Yeah, I'm mulling & mulling. Mad mullin.'"

It struck me that to get an accurate read on how I should end this novel I should go back to the beginning and read through it as far as I could before Maren got here. I went back to the beginning and read. I read through page 74. Lena hooked up with Tank and told Mira about it in 2004.

Maren came over on May 22, 2016. We sat in my museum-like living room full of oil paintings and antiques. Two withered red roses from the *Purple Rain* screening at in water on my coffee table. I ordered pizza thinking we could both have some. Maren said she couldn't eat the cheese. I stuffed myself with veggie pizza before she came over then put it away in my refrigerator.

I brewed coffee. Drank cup after cup of coffee as I talked to Maren. She railed against Melody who was trying to breakup her marriage. I sympathized. We watched *The Big Lebowski* in the background.

Around one am Maren left. I smoked a bowl. Keurig-brewed a cup of coffee. Got back to the *Angelina at the Serrano* manuscript. I read up to page 103. Lena, Ben, Angelina and Mira traveled to San Francisco. The overhead light in my apartment flickered on and off. I lay on the couch in my blue feather-edged bathrobe typing madly.

I went back to page 103. Echo Park, again. Cradle of my years of love with Katie. I knew I would have to edit *Katie Rising* again and again before to would be done. Possibly next. It takes a very long time to do this sort of work.

Suddenly it was 3:51 am. I went through my old hard drive for hours grafting bits of text to *Angelina at the Serrano*, *Scaffolding* and *Katie Rising*. It did not seem like I was going to get any sleep tonight. A cockroach watched me from the printer as I sat at the IKEA desk struggling with fragments. Finding new homes for scraps of text.

The roses from the *Purple Rain* screening scented the air. I exhaled a bowl of weed. Heard voices talking outside quietly in the night. I couldn't tell if they were my psychosis or a real conversation overheard on the dimly lit Hollywood street. In someone's car. In LACC across the street. In the quiet of the night.

I knew that up here in my apartment I was safe and comfortable. Five locks, two gates, a door and a stair stood between me and the outside world. Whatever I was overhearing could stay out there.

I listening to the enormous quiet of the night. Heard an airplane drone far away. A car revved. Pulled away. I listened to the silence. It was 4:14 am.

I could smell the roses. They smelled beautiful. I reminder the L'Occitaine Rose Milk that I bought first in San Francisco while hanging out with Brady and Lucas in 2004. I fell in love with my delicate disco rose perfume.

Katie's mother, my mother-in-law, gifted me another bottle of rose milk in Christmas 2010. I stayed in touch with my in-laws after the death. I was so thankful for their kindness. I still had that bottle of rose milk.

I went back to my bedroom to put some on. It was time to smell like roses. I wanted to bathe in roses. I rose, dripping blue feathers. Went into the bathroom carrying my laptop. I wondered if anyone knew or cared that I was still awake. Probably not, it didn't seem.

I tolerated my neighbors afterparties and electric guitars and they tolerated my solitude, nocturnal lifestyle and unwillingness to share my weed. Peaceful co-existence in that Hollywood apartment after so many difficult living situations of the past.

I turned the living room light off as I went. Turned the hall light off. Left the kitchen light off to keep the cockroaches down to a dull roar. Moved carrying my laptop to the bedroom.

I turned off the light as I entered the bedroom. Picked up the L'Occitaine rose milk. Shook out an ample dollop. Smoothed it all over my body. I bathed in rose milk. Climbed inside my bed. Pulled first the Urban Outfitters watercolor flower duvet over me then the burgundy sheet.

I was a blanket fort smelling of roses.

My slim silver Macbook came to life suddenly. I put in my earbuds to hear my iTunes playing Adult.'s *Resusitation*. My iTunes came on at random playing San Francisco disco hits while I was wrote *Angelina at the Serrano*. I took it as a good sign. I wondered if I wrote about the act of writing too much. Wrote too much about my other unpublished and possibly unpublishable novels

Depending on when you're reading this book right now. As you finish the final pages. As you prepare to set it down. Go read the others if they have been released yet because they exist. Even if only on my hard drive waiting to be born.

Adult's "Skinlike" came on my headphones. Then "Private Conversations."

I pulled back the sheet. Flowers. rose milk. Blanket fort. The absolute present of May 22, 2016 4:33 am that became the past as soon as it was uttered. I wondered if I felt a cockroach crawling on my blue nylon back. My spine poked through the net robe.

I sat in my blanket fort. It was 5:54 am Sunday morning. It struck me that outside the blanket fort it must be dawn. What better time to do yoga. Meditate. Drink a piping hot cup of coffee. Stretch my neck and back.

I rose. Threw off the coverlet. The cold air whooshed in. Austria's "Darken Her Horse" came on my iTunes. It was dawn. Magic hour. I could hear the birds chirping. Yes, time to take a break. Get some coffee. I turned off the iTunes.

I moved my computer and charge cord into the shifting brightening living room. I could hear people talking on the street. The whir of a bicycle passing. My curtains were bright with dawn. I went to make a cup of coffee.

I hurried through yoga and meditation. Got a bunch of new ideas for previously written text to put into my novels during yoga. Finished meditation. Snuffed the incense. It was so nice to always have incense to meditate with since I started snuffing it when I was done. I rushed back to my laptop with the coffee.

The first project was beginning a new book about the future. I called it "Los Angeles After the Apocalypse." It was a book I had yet to write in May 2016. I would finish it later at some point in the future. The apocalypse hadn't happened yet so I couldn't write it yet. Would I still have a laptop and iCloud storage if the apocalypse happened? Probably not. Yet I hopefully assemble the previously published text.

I combined three futuristic post-apocalyptic things I'd previously published for *Los Angeles After the Apocalypse*. Didn't even cut chapters or change tenses because I had told myself in theory that I wasn't allowed to start any more books until I finished and published the ones I was working on. Here I was starting new books after all but it had to be done. Tentative book fetuses only. I was laying the groundwork's for my life's work.

I closed the document before breaking it into chapters. Set the novel fetus aside for another day. I had the rest of my life to finish and publish these books. Hopefully I would live long enough to do it. I was trying.

I began to get hungry.

I got up and got a piece of veggie pizza from the large pizza sitting in my refrigerator. Cure for my imaginary anorexia. It would sustain me while I worked on my novel. The cat jumped down off the desk and on the table. She chewed at the rose leaves in the vase. I got another piece of pizza. Ate on the couch. It was a serviceable cold slice of veggie pizza. Nothing worth writing Entropy food essays like "Eating My Way Back," about but nourishing. I gnawed the crust. Ate one more piece of cold pizza standing up in the kitchen while brewing one more cup of coffee. When I pulled all-nighters like this coffee was essential.

I was supposed to go over to Bobby's later as I so often timed my all-nighters so as to be able to go to sleep when he did at nine pm. I would just stay up the entire night previous. Many times we had the best times ever when I was sleep deprived. I would fall asleep blissfully on his shoulder with Saphris under my tongue as I hoped to tonight.

At 8 am May 22, 2016 I sipped my coffee. Considered the day ahead. I had my work cut out for me. I had a lot of work to do today. I wanted to make it through *Angelina at the Serrano* again with all of the new additions at the end. I wanted to see if it all flowed together.

I went back to where I left off earlier in the night previous. Chapter 12. Page 115. The gang in Los Angeles on vacay. Swimming at the Standard Hotel. I wanted to understand my past to come through to my future. I fixed chapter numbering again. Skimmed through the whole document.

I read through all of *Angelina at the Serrano* until I got to the end. Updated the playlist. Read over the text I wrote that moment in my rose scented blanket fort. It was good.

As I was finishing up, Lish called. We talked rapidly about her impressions of Bobby on our double date. The fact that she was breaking up with Roland soon. Her desire to go out with me and Maren and have a girl's night. Being as Maren was stewing in the failure of her marriage and Lish in the end of her relationship, joining forces seemed like a good idea.

By the time I severed with Lish I was glad I hadn't introduced her to Maren as much as Lish wanted to meet Maren because I didn't want my two only friends to close forces behind me and exclude me. As well as I knew Lish I also knew what she in her millennials toxicity was capable of. I kept what boundaries I had to enforce with her until I finally had to move on.

My phone call with Lish was interrupted by Bobby's call. He said he's been gypped by the garage door opener company that charged him $600 to fix his garage door. He was upset. Before he could tell me when to come over, he dropped my call to take another call.

I considered calling Lish back. Made another cup of coffee. Finished up reading through the manuscript.

When I got to the end I realized that twelve years of my life were encapsulated here. I had made it through twelve years of dramatic changed from the depths of addiction to healthy California sober recovery.

Angelina at the Serrano was the novel that Bruce Bauman wanted me to write at CalArts instead of druggie *Jet Set Desolate*. Bauman wanted me to write a druggie San Francisco novel where the character gets sober at the end. Considering so much of this book was written and outlined at CalArts I think I was writing this book then but didn't know it yet.

Twelve years. Dramatic changes. So many friends, lovers and frenemies lost to time. Other books written or to write.

Time passes, inexorably.

Twelve years. 2004-2016.

Mira and Tank were lost to time and probably jail. Angelina was in Amsterdam with her online magazine. Limone was settled in the Bay Area with her daughter and cheating husband. Micah was my friend on Facebook. He posted often. I was always so relieved to find that he wasn't dead of AIDS.

Curtis was dead. Brady was dead. Katie was dead. The death toll mounted as the casualties piled. But some of us were still alive. Was it a blessing or a curse to still be alive with these memories?

Maren was still alive mulling over the possible end of her marriage in Los Angeles. Omar was still alive settling in in Miami. Bobby was probably moving in with his parents after being out of work for too long. Renting out his ambitious Mount Washington home. Lish was making new best friends with an homeless model with a motorcycle and a bulldog who talked her ear off in Urban Outfitters and wanted to go to bars with her when I did not.

I saw Lish's posts about her new best friend on Facebook.

Thought, "Godspeed girl. I didn't want you to suffer any more than I already knew you were."

I am not cruel. I do not wish to cause undue suffering. I seek healing. Ihope that all the other wounded souls that have crosses my path, then diverged from it , find their healing as well.

I got up in June 2016 to shit out the coffee that I had been drinking all morning. Dropped blue feathers on my way to the bathroom. I brought my iPhone to the toilet. Looked at the Mint App. The $7,209 in my checking account and $32,206 in investments looked awfully sweet. It was nice to not be as poor as I was in 2004-2014. It was nice to see a private psychiatrist and therapist. It was nice to be able to afford all the weed I wanted to smoke.

Must be nice. It was.

Bobby called me back to make up. He said that he felt I didn't have his back enough and didn't help him enough. I promised to help him more in the future. We made plans to work out together that night then possibly go see the LA Drones at the Echoplex. He told me to come over at five pm. Looking at my iCal I decided to take my afternoon Klonopin and Trileptal.

I decided to get another Venti Caramel Cone Frappuccino from the drive-through Starbucks on York on the way to Bobby's house. Delicious. I lived for Frappuccino's in early 2016 until I cut that expensive habit out like the rest. I felt like I needed the dairy in the whipped cream. They were like a sundae for emaciated me. I decided that on the way to gaining enough weigh back not to be anorexic anymore I ought to drink as many Frappuccino's as I wanted.

What to wear tonight? It really was almost time to get ready. I was supposed to bathe at Bobby's after working out. Come over wearing something sporty yet have on reserve something to wear to a show. Okay.

I picked up my laptop. Went into the bedroom to get ready. Smeared my new body with coconut oil. Spritzed Foreign Exchange perfume that Lish gave me once. I was over at her house and she was cleaning out old makeup.

Lish gave me so many beautiful things because she had poor boundaries. I gave her a collage of her modeling photos, a Benefit Do the Hoola Liquid Bronzer and a copy of *Jet Set Desolate*. I gave people gifts on birthdays and Christmas. Not incidentally and periodically whenever I came over as she did.

Bobby gave me lavish gifts too. Lish and Bobby gave me many gifts that I still kept and wore after they exited my life out of both sentimentality and thriftiness. I understood the value of things having lost before so much.

The crucial rift between Lish and I happened August 2016 when we stayed up all night talking on the phone as we so often did. Lish told me that things and money didn't matter at all to her as she was dying.

I knew I would live for a lot longer then Lish. I needed to hold on to my things and money so that they would last my whole life. I could no longer go out with Lish as I had gone out with Angelina, Mira, Limone, Lucas and Brady so long ago unless I wanted to end up back in San Diego again or in and out of more institutions.

I wanted to stay solvent and stable in Los Angeles. I had to get out of the friendship with Lish before she destroyed me. This way I wouldn't have to watch her die.

What to wear? What leggings and a top combo would I dial up today? Should I actually wear a dress? Nah. We were supposed to work out. Bobby said wear something sporty. I pulled on the cold-weather snowflake leggings Bobby gave me and an old wife-beater that had belonged to José. Finding the perfect leggings for any given situation was about what getting dressed had come to for me.

What jacket? One of the Adidas sports jackets? Nah. We might be going out later. I pulled on the cropped leather jacket that I bought in 2004 in San Francisco.

When I brought that leather jacket home from the vintage boutique on Haight Street Angelina said, "I have one just like that, Lena." I still wore it all the time now that Angelina was lost to the sands of time. She stole my cat ear hoodie anyway.

I plowed through heaps of jewelry looking for the perfect necklace for my sporty rocker outfit. Untangled an Urban Outfitters sunburst necklace that would work. Carefully put it on with a black stone two-finger ring. A black leather studded bracelet. The silver chain bracelet Lish gave me that I wore all the time.

Now for makeup. Getting ready seemed so tedious all of a sudden. But if I got it over with quick I could write for a little while longer. I put on MAC palette Contouring. Highlighter palette. Neutral eye makeup. Pink gloss. Mascara.

I went back into the living room. Sat down heavily on the couch. I packed up my pot. Put the eighth, the pipe and three lighters into the green cloth bag I transported it in. Put the bag in my orange leather American Apparel clutch purse.

In twelve year I was still the same flawed, mentally ill woman. California sober now instead of a desperate drug addict. Glad I was no longer picking grains of meth of the floor of cheap hotel rooms while Tank waited in the bed.

I rolled up my pink leopard yoga mat. Put away my Little Miss Sunshine mug and the cut glass tumbler on the coffee table. Zipped up my boots.

I sallied forth to Bobby's to take what adventure came. As I had in San Francisco before.

THE END

www.ingramcontent.com/pod-product-compliance
Lightning Source LLC
LaVergne TN
LVHW041217150826
845673LV00001B/441

* 9 7 8 8 1 1 9 6 5 4 3 7 6 *